Multidimensional Peace

Multidimensional Peace

Quiet In Stern, Calm In Storm

By

Ikechukwu J. Madumere

Nukan Publishing

Multidimensional Peace

(Quiet In Stern, Calm In Storm)

by Ikechukwu J. Madumere

ISBN: **978-1-9161489-1-8**

Published by **Nukan Publishing**
Essex UK
Email: admin@nukan.com

First Printed in **United Kingdom** 2025

Cover designed by **Creative Brain**

ENDORSEMENTS

"This is a profound and timely masterpiece that offers a holistic approach to achieving inner peace amidst the daily unrest that confronts us on our life's journey. The author's insightful words are a balm to the soul. Using the Scriptures, he guides the readers on a transformative journey of self-discovery, healing, and spiritual growth. This book is a must-read for anyone seeking to cultivate multidimensional peace because it encompasses the emotional, mental, physical, and spiritual aspects of life. The author's wisdom, compassion, and expertise sparkle through every page of the book, thereby making it a valuable resource for individuals from all walks of life.

I highly recommend this *"Multidimensional Peace"* to anyone seeking to navigate life's challenges with greater ease and resilience. The message is both uplifting and empowering, offering a beacon of hope in these uncertain times."

Bishop Benjamin Ameh Enwuchola
Bishop, Anglican Diocese of Otukpo
Benue State, Nigeria.

***

"A profound and inspiring exploration of peace in all its dimensions. The author's blend of biblical wisdom, personal stories, and practical guidance makes this a must-read for anyone seeking true inner peace."

Pastor Anthony Ijeh
Associate Pastor, The Redeemed Christian Church of God
Canterbury, Kent, United Kingdom.

"Peace is artificial. Anarchy is the default state of nature. Anarchy is a creation of random energy. Absence of energy will lead to absolute peace, the peace of the graveyard! This kind of peace is not desirable because nothing can be achieved in death! Therefore, there must of a necessity, be energy. Unfortunately, as energy (riches, influence, authority, knowledge, technology etc.) increases, the degree of disorderliness (entropy) increases as well. Therefore, if one desires peace, he must learn to manage energy. Energy must be available and released in controllable proportions. This state will engender the peace that brings fulfilment. It takes deliberate effort to create and sustain peace.

In this book, *Multidimensional Peace,* Dr Ikechukwu Madumere seeks to equip the reader with the requisite life and lifestyle that create and allow peace to reign. The mechanisms presented here are born out of spirit guided life experiences and studies and I find them practicable.

Dr Madumere is a practicing peace advocate who has influenced many of us by his exemplary living. Putting his thoughts on paper is a way of reaching a wider audience. The book is so enriching and I endorse it for all. Do get a copy."

Rev. Canon Dr Okafor J. Chinedu
Rector of the Anglican Mission Hospital, TAMH
Parish Priest, St. Barnabas' Church
Keffi, Nigeria.

***

"Having gone through this book, *MULTIDIMENSIONAL PEACE* I see Dr Madumere walking us through the lens of scriptures and his personal, family, and secular relational experiences. He defined peace as one of the most prized possessions everyone needs in life and has put together his personal lessons that have helped him live a peaceful life even in challenging times. Dr

Madumere believes that peace of mind is an overarching panacea for living an all -round fulfilling life. For his love for God and fellow human beings he has in this book in your hand painstakingly put together pitfalls that can stifle peace.

The aim of making this book available in your hand is for you to learn and adapt to enhance your life as you pursue peace with all. I recommend *MULTIDIMENSIONAL PEACE* to you."

Maria Chika Amadi
Pastor | Author | Legal Adviser | former elected UK Councillor
London, United Kingdom

***

"*Multidimensional Peace* by Dr Madumere is a timely and insightful guide to cultivating inner calm and relational harmony in an often chaotic world. Drawing from biblical principles and life's practical realities, the book offers a deeply thoughtful, faith-based roadmap to maintaining peace across all areas of life. With clarity and compassion, Dr Madumere equips readers with tools to navigate conflict, strengthen relationships, and guard their hearts and minds. A must-read for anyone seeking lasting peace and emotional well-being in today's fast-paced world."

Dr Etiowo Ekanem
(MD, MRCGP, DRCOG, CCFP, PgCert Med Ed)
Family Physician
Canada

***

"*Multidimensional Peace* is spirit-breathed manual that affirms peace as both divine nature and gift (John 14:27, Ephesians 2:14). With the engaging storytelling of lived experiences, it echoes contemporary truths like: 'Peace is a conscious choice' and 'Peace is not the absence of trouble, but the presence of Christ'. Each chapter is a layered deep insight into peace with God, with self, and with others in three (multi-) dimensions. Very importantly, the reader's mind is illuminated to the reality that without God Almighty (what may be called the Supreme Dimension), peace cannot exist in the other two dimensions (self and others). Dr Ik's depiction of Jesus asleep in the stern offers a compelling metaphor for resting in God amidst life's storms. This book is not just to be read—it is to be practiced. I wholeheartedly commend it to all who seek true rest in a restless world."

Dr Chuka Onaga
(MBBS, MBA, MPH, Diploma HIV Management)
Independent Global Health Consultant
Chief of Party at Right To Care Non-Profit Company
Nelspruit, South Africa.

***

"*MULTIDIMENSIONAL PEACE: QUIET IN STERN, CALM IN STORM* gives a great exposition to the fundamentals and different facets of peace within our innermost self, our homes and the society. Dr Madumere once again has demonstrated his uncanny ability to delve into such a complex but basic aspect of humanity and simplify it for general application in different aspects of our lives. It is a great read and I highly recommend it!"

Dr Jude C. Eze, FWACP, FRCPCH
Consultant Paediatrician
Newcastle, United Kingdom.

***

"This work offers a profound and timely exploration of peace and spirituality. Across its twelve thoughtfully structured chapters — from defining peace and exploring the peace of God, to understanding peace with God, the ABCs of peace, and practical 'peace boosters' – the author guides the reader with both clarity and compassion. Each chapter builds not only knowledge but also spiritual resonance, making this book a companion for both reflection and transformation. I wholeheartedly endorse this work and believe it will serve as a meaningful resource for all who seek to cultivate a deeper, more grounded experience of peace in their lives and communities."

Dr. Bonaventure A. Egbujie, MD, MPH, PhD
Implementation and Research Scientist, Toronto Grace Health Centre
Adjunct Professor, School of Public Health Sciences, University of Waterloo,
Ontario, Canada

***

"Multidimensional Peace is a divinely inspired guide to the deep, abiding peace that only God can give. It takes the reader through a sacred journey that transcends theory and portrays peace as a lived, spiritual, and emotional reality. Dr. Madumere weaves together heartfelt personal stories, scriptural wisdom, and practical insights that reveal the stillness of Christ in every storm and the serenity that flows from a heart anchored in Him. Each chapter gently urges the reader toward wholeness, healing, and harmony with self, God, and others. A truly transformative read for anyone seeking serenity in a turbulent world."

Dr Judith Obinna-Keke
Lecturer-in-Law at South Bank University,
London, United Kingdom.

***

"Peace is the bedrock or platform on which prosperity thrives, meaning the absence of peace then prosperity will be truncated. *Multidimensional Peace* authored by Dr Joshua Madumere, gives us very tangible insight into the various ways we can have peace within (inner peace) and without (family, workplace, community and nation - outer peace). This book also made a deeper dive into how we can maintain our God-given peace in crisis situations, that is, to be quiet in a stern and calm in a storm. Without much rhetoric, I humbly recommend this book to all, as a must-read."

Pastor Ebenezer Ayokunle
Parish Pastor of The Redeemed Christian Church of God, Holy Ghost Zone,
Canterbury, United Kingdom.

***

"*Multidimensional Peace* is a thoughtful and enriching read. It radiates deep wisdom and reveals the author's multidimensional identity—as a devoted son of God, a loving husband and father, and a medical professional committed to holistic well-being. Through accessible reflections and scriptural insights, the book invites readers into a life anchored in purpose and discernment of the different facets of peace—a truly uplifting contribution to the pursuit of peace in our personal and shared lives."

Dr Ohio Omiunu
City of David Canterbury and University of Kent.
United Kingdom

DEDICATION

To my esteemed wife, Angel, for your care and respect; for embodying peace in our union and for your unwavering dedication to our joint responsibilities of home-keeping and the principles of love throughout our journey from the beginning.

To my wonderful children: Joshua, David, Chidalu & Chizara for the blessing of your presence in our family.

To my late father, Chief Christian Madumere, and my mother, Mrs Monica Madumere, for your love and for nurturing me toward fulfilling God's purpose for my life.

To my siblings: Obiageri, Chinazo, Ogochukwu, Izuchukwu, and Odinaka for your love and for being my dream siblings.

To the entire Madumere family, I extend my heartfelt gratitude for your love and care.

To Aunty Christie, for serving as a pivotal figure in my journey to the UK.

To my amazing friends, colleagues, supporters, and every lover and proponent of global peace.

To City of David Canterbury, my spiritual families far and near, and my spiritual parents for your prayers.

ACKNOWLEDGEMENTS

I would like to sincerely thank those who have significantly helped this work and influenced my development in inspired writing. My deepest thanks go to God, who is the actual originator and finisher of this vision.

To my dear wife, I acknowledge your love and priceless contributions to this work. I appreciate your support during my late nights at the computer. I would also like to extend my sincere gratitude to our amazing children - Joshua, David, Caleb, and Chizara. It is my hope that this book will bring blessings to you in all aspects of your life experiences.

To my parents, Chief Christian Madumere (late) and Mrs. Monica Madumere, your love has profoundly influenced who I am today—thank you. To my siblings, Oby, Chinazo, Ogochukwu, Izuna, and Odinaka, I am grateful for your unwavering support and affection. I would like to extend my sincere gratitude to my aunt, Mrs. Christie Ikeogu, for her generous support in facilitating my migration to the United Kingdom. I extend my thanks to my parents-in-law, Sir and Lady Cajetan Okolo, for their relentless support. A special thanks to The Reverend and Mrs. Constantine and Faith Osuchukwu in Ballarat, Australia, for their prayers.

My heartfelt thanks go to Bishop Benjamin Ameh Enwuchola, Pastor Anthony Ijeh, Rev. Canon Dr Okafor J. Chinedu, Maria Chika Amadi, Dr Etiowo Ekanem, Dr Chuka Onaga, Dr Jude C. Eze, Dr Bonaventure A. Egbujie, Dr Judith Obinna-Keke, Pastor Ebenezer Ayokunle, and Dr Ohio Omiunu, for giving up part of their time to read and review the book. I thank you all for your kind endorsements.

I would like to extend my sincere gratitude to Pastor Akin Kunlipe and Pastor Tony Ijeh of City of David, Canterbury, as well as Pastor Akinkumi Thomas of Living Bread, Newcastle, for their exemplary leadership and teachings, which have provided invaluable spiritual insights for this work. I wish to also extend my sincere gratitude to Apostle George Amadi, Founder of Goodnews Church, London, for his spiritual guidance in my life. I would like to acknowledge the members, leaders, and brethren of the Overseas Fellowship of Nigerian Christians, Kent Branch, for their encouragement and support, which have been vital for his work.

My gratitude also goes to Dr (Mrs.) N. Dandam, Chief Lecturer and Senior Pastor at La Paix Christian Mission International, Jos Nigeria, for her foundational role in my Christian journey. I would like to express my profound gratitude to my younger brothers, Izuchukwu Madumere and Barrister Nelson Madumere (Ph.D.), for their family support in the UK during this work and always. Due to space constraints, I would like to globally acknowledge the support, encouragement, and well-wishes of my medical colleagues, classmates, and friends, both near and far.

I am especially grateful to everyone who recommends this book as a peace manual, particularly Pastor Akin Kunlipe, Lead Pastor at City of David, Canterbury, for writing the foreword.

May we find peace with God and experience peace of God in every part of our lives, work, and relationships. Amen.

Blessings,
Dr Ikechukwu Joshua Madumere

Contents

ENDORSEMENTS....................vii

DEDICATION....................xiii

ACKNOWLEDGEMENTS....................xiv

FOREWORD....................xvii

PREFACE....................xix

Chapter 1: PEACE DEFINED....................25

Chapter 2: THE BACKGROUND AND THE CHOICES....................35

Chapter 3: QUIET IN STERN; CALM IN STORM....................43

Chapter 4: THE PEACE OF GOD....................77

Chapter 5: PEACE WITH GOD....................89

Chapter 6: THE ABC OF ENDURING PEACE....................95

Chapter 7: THE PEACE WITHIN - INNER PEACE WITH YOURSELF....................109

Chapter 8: INTERPERSONAL RELATIONSHIPS - PEACE WITH MAN....................127

Chapter 9: IT ALL STARTS WITH FOUNDATION....................141

Chapter 10: YOUR LIGHT SHINES WHEREVER YOU GO....................149

Chapter 11: LITTLE AND BIG PEACE BOOSTERS....................155

Chapter 12: PEACE ON ALL SIDES....................165

REFERENCES....................171

ABOUT THE AUTHOR....................173

RESOURCES FROM THE AUTHOR....................174

FOREWORD

A cursory look on an internet search engine suggests that there may be anywhere between a dozen to fifty armed conflicts around the world today. This number is made up of the wars and conflicts that make the news, as well as the little-known conflicts that are just as disruptive and destructive as the well-publicised ones.

No search engine however, will be completely able to put a number to the conflicts that individuals of all generations, marriages, families, relationships, work places, businesses, governments, even churches may be facing at any one time.

The reality is that conflicts are an inevitable part of life. There is an enemy who pits man against God and man against his fellow man. The enemy's relentless work against peace is the source of conflict.

All this makes peace one of the most precious and sought after commodities in this world. We need *MULTIDIMENSIONAL PEACE.*

In this well-researched and well-written book, Dr Ikechukwu Joshua Madumere draws on personal lessons on peace. He leans heavily on the word of God as revealed in the Bible to provide this insightful and practical "peace manual".

Dr Madumere carefully sets out how peace, multidimensional peace is available to all, despite the inevitability of conflict.

I am glad to commend this wonderful book to you and encourage that you approach it is as a valuable resource for bringing a peace that passes all understanding into your life and all your relationships.

May God bless you with multidimensional peace as you read.

Pastor Akin Kunlipe
Lead Pastor at RCCG City of David, Canterbury, UK

PREFACE

What is life without peace, and what are life's achievements or successes without the comfort and serenity of a tranquil heart or soul? Peace of mind is one of man's most prized possessions. In the absence of peace, life shifts from an experience intended for enjoyment to one characterized by mere endurance, often involving a frantic pursuit of unproductive activities.

It is recognized that human actions, relationships, behaviours, words, professional decisions, investments, feelings, experiences, ambitions, and aspirations are consciously or unconsciously influenced by man's desire to attain, maintain, or enhance peace. Peace encompasses various dimensions within human experiences, with spirituality serving as its foundation. Therefore, for life to be rewarding and enjoyable in all aspects, it is essential to avoid being drawn into unnecessary or preventable conflicts that steal your peace by external circumstances or individuals. Instead, strive to pull others and situations into your state of peace through your actions and reactions.

When the Lord spoke to me regarding this work leading up to my 50th birthday, He assured that if I remain faithful to Him in pursuing what matters, that He will guarantee me a new level of peace with life of ease in the next phase of my life. This was following an experience where I was worried about several things

I wanted to achieve before turning 50, some of which were still outstanding leading up to this landmark anniversary, including, early retirement plan. The Lord then opened my eyes about what matters most – the gift of salvation and where he picked me to where I am now - in Him. God showed me both major and minor things that stifle peace, with inspiration to put them in writing to benefit others. I shared this revelation with my supportive wife and children during our 2024 New Year resolutions, with a view to start soon, but the loss of my father meant I could not progress as planned. My father's illness and subsequent passing was challenging, as were the demanding responsibilities of funeral planning and addressing the void his death created. My father's expression of submission to God for the salvation of his soul before his passing, together with the spirit-inspired exceptional sense of calm I prayerfully encountered amidst multiple trials and tests of faith during this difficult period, would ultimately help me to affirm *Multidimensional Peace* as the title of this work. I am persuaded that God called my father home for his peace, to the Glory of His name.

By utilising truth, principles, and relatable human and compelling scriptural examples, this book aims to demonstrate that a genuinely peaceful life is one that is experienced in multiple dimensions: in significant matters and minor ones; during favourable times and challenging periods. It seeks to guide readers on how to create peace when it depends on their actions and how to maintain peace of mind through spirit-inspired thoughts and edifying reactions, when it does not entirely depend on them.

Defined by Cambridge dictionary as "freedom from war or violence," peace further explains a "state of not being interrupted or annoyed by worries, problems, noise or unwanted actions. "

This definition, therefore, implies at least, two pathways to peace:

- Peace derived from absence of peace disruptors like worriers.
- Peace derived from proper handling of peace disruptors, or appropriate reaction to them when they occur.

Beyond physical considerations, this work presents a concrete scriptural demonstration of peace as a gift from God, that is then shared with humans through virtuous relationships in our families, communities, workplaces and social environments, to create a peaceful world.

One of the anchor scriptures used here, the book of Philippians 4:6-8 will give us an empowering insight on peace. It says:

"Don't worry about anything; instead, pray about everything. Tell God what you need and thank him for all he has done. Then you will experience God's peace, which exceeds anything we can understand. His peace will guard your hearts and minds as you live in Christ Jesus. And now, dear brothers and sisters, one final thing. Fix your thoughts on what is true, and honourable, and right, and pure, and lovely, and admirable. Think about things that are excellent and worthy of praise. Keep putting into practice all you learned and received from me—everything you heard from me and saw me doing. Then the God of peace will be with you." (Philippians 4: 6-9 NLT).

Following simple introductory definition of peace with practical examples in the first Chapter, an insightful background in chapter two, based partly on personal experience, leads smoothly to an enthralling story of a restfully sleeping and peaceful Christ in the stern amid the storm on the Galilean sea, that got His disciples panicked and bereft of peace. This example of Christ's peace, despite many external disruptions, highlights a powerful and complex scriptural model of multidimensional peace that forms the basis of this work. From the concept of peace of God in Chapter 4 to Peace with God in Chapter 5, I made efforts to explain the nature and source of multidimensional peace. I also placed emphasis on its supernatural foundation, connection, and attributes, with Christ at the centre, as both the provider and embodiment of peace.

When Ronald Reagan described peace as "not the absence of conflicts, but the ability to manage conflicts by peaceful means", he points us to the inevitability of conflicts in life. Therefore, given that "we find peace not by trying to escape problems, but by confronting them courageously and not though denial, but in victory," according to Donald Walters, chapter 6, the ABC of peace, presents a behavioural template that is systematically intended to help us manage disrupters of peace when they occur, by guiding our reactions to difficulties and adversities, with empowering peace outcomes for all involved.

Achieving peace in the external world requires first attaining inner peace. Chapter 7 emphasizes this point, presenting inner peace as essential for achieving broader peace. Chapters 8 to 11 then address interpersonal relationships and peace-building efforts, highlighting the role of edifying home training as the foundation for virtues and values that support peace within communities and societies, beginning with families.

I concluded this work by emphasizing the importance of achieving, sustaining or increasing peace through optimising both minor and significant peace-promoting actions called peace boosters as well as discourse on the significance of peace on all sides. As dedicated ambassadors of peace, it is imperative that we strive to make a positive impact on our world.

It is my earnest intention and hope that this book offers you enduring peace, positively influencing your personal life, relationships, and daily experiences, whatever challenges, or successes you may encounter.

While it is my prayer that the Lord blesses you with countless nuggets in this book as you read, one inspired revelation may be all you need from it for God to change the course of your relationships, job or family for good. May you not miss it.

Amen.

Chapter 1
PEACE DEFINED

PEACE is one of the most important words in our world and relationships, comparable in importance (in relationships), only to justice, which provides solid foundation for enduring peace through conflict prevention, and love, which is an essential requirement for a lasting peace both within individuals and between groups.

This chapter starts with a simple dictionary definition of peace, leading to scriptural perspectives for a holistic and empowering understanding.

Peace is defined by the Cambridge dictionary in several ways, two of which are pertinent for this work.

A) PEACE IS "FREEDOM FROM WAR AND VIOLENCE, ESPECIALLY WHEN PEOPLE LIVE AND WORK TOGETHER HAPPILY, WITHOUT DISAGREEMENTS."

Examples:

- *He wants to enjoy his meal in peace.*
- *David enjoyed a reign of peace as king of Israel.*

- *He is a man of peace, and she is very good at **keeping** (the) peace within the family.*
- *They will be having a peace talk next week.*

Comment:

This definition describes an ideal world without war or disagreement, a higher level of peace. While this seems utopian from a human perspective, spiritually, with God all things are possible (Luke 1:37 NKJV).

Using the words "peace" and "rest" interchangeably, the scripture presents King David as a beneficiary of this kind of peace:

"When King David lived in his house (palace) and the Lord had given him rest from all his surrounding enemies," (2 Samuel 7:1 AMP).

During Joshua's leadership of the Israelite people, the period of peace was scripturally recorded as follows:

"The Lord gave them peace throughout the land, just as he had promised their ancestors. Not one of all their enemies had been able to stand against them, because the Lord gave the Israelites the victory over all their enemies." (Joshua 21:44 GNT).

Achieving this level of peace requires supernatural grace - to remain calm and content despite external factors, people, or circumstances that may cause conflicts even if you have done everything correctly.

God therefore has an indispensable role to play in your peace to make people and situations be at peace with you.

"The king's heart is in the hand of the Lord, Like the rivers of water; He turns it wherever He wishes." (Proverbs 21:1 NKJV)

At human level also, you have a duty to maintain peace with others, even with those who may want conflict. Your enemies can be at peace with you when the Lord is on your side.

"When a man's ways please the Lord, He makes even his enemies to be at peace with him." (Proverbs 16:7 NKJV).

Therefore, for this type of peace:

- You need supernatural assistance. You need to pray and seek help from God. The good news is; this HELP is available:
  "God is our Refuge and Strength [mighty *and* impenetrable to temptation], a very present *and* well-proved help in trouble." (Psalm 46:1 AMPC).
- Your ways and actions should please the Lord, including how you relate to Him and treat others. And GRACE for this is also available:
  "Therefore, let us [with privilege] approach the throne of grace [that is, the throne of God's gracious favour] with confidence and without fear, so that we may receive mercy [for our failures] and find [His amazing] grace to help in time of need [an appropriate blessing, coming just at the right moment]." (Hebrews 4:16 AMP).

And when you live your life in pursuit of God's purpose (which includes peace with both God and man), He will turn your weaknesses to strengths, and transform your mess into a message, by renewing your mind to fulfil what is consistent with His Good, Acceptable and PERFECT will (Romans 12:1-2).

Because you work with and deal with humans and things outside your control daily, you need to connect with God to help you have peace at this level.

B) **PEACE IS "THE STATE OF NOT BEING INTERRUPTED OR ANNOYED BY WORRY, PROBLEMS, NOISE, OR UNWANTED ACTIONS."**

Examples:

- *You need peace to live a truly healthy life.*
- *You'll need peace **and quiet** to study.*
- *Go away and leave us to finish our dinner **in** peace.*
- *For your peace of mind, go back and check that you locked the door.*
- *There'll be **no** peace until everyone gets what he or she wants.*
- *I actually disagreed with what she said but I held my peace (did not say anything).*

Comment:

The interruptions, annoyance, worries, problems, noise, or unwanted actions that violate peace are usually not transient ones with no impact on people's ways and life. For them to affect your peace usually means they matter to you; they target your mind through which they affect your emotional comfort and destabilise your sense of ease.

This aspect of peace touches on you and what you do in relation to the things that happen to you, and around you.

The focus here, however, is not on those peace-breaching factors (noise, problems, annoying experiences or unwanted actions) that happen to you or around you, but on your role in triggering them and/or how you handle, manage or respond to them once they have happened. This kind of peace is covered in:

- Your actions and lifestyle choices crucial for maintaining your mental and physical health, to ensure long-term well-being and peace.
- What you do and the decisions you take to keep yourself out of a toxic, unhealthy environment of war and out of avoidable, damaging exchanges or disagreements.
- What you do to create a positive and healthy atmosphere at home preparatory to, or during events, like your exam, your spouse's birthday anniversary or during a family holiday - so that these events are seamlessly enjoyed with happy memories.
- What you do in your relationship(s) so that everyone appropriately gets what he or she appropriately desires and needs, in order that you all win together and be happy together. What affects one in a relationship affects the other and until you win with love and justice in relationship, you cannot have peace.

Charles R. Swindoll writes: ***"Life is 10% What Happens to You and 90% How You React."***

Marcus Aurelius in seeming agreement asserts: ***"If you are distressed by anything external, the pain is not due to the thing itself but to your own estimate of it; and this you have the power to revoke at any moment."***

In harmony with Mr Swindoll's powerful quote, I personally agree that 10% of the times, our peace is about what happens to us, and 90% of the times, our peace is determined by how we manage them, and this depends on who you are and what is inside of you.

You can therefore guarantee 90% of your peace by:

- Reacting to people's disappointing behaviours or shortcomings in ways and manners that are corrective, and yet healthy for relationships, at home or workplaces, and in social situations where you deal with and manage people (Ephesians 4:15-16, 25-26 NKJV).
- Responding to adversities with a positive attitude and mindset, coupled with discernment and wisdom, which is crucial for safeguarding one's mental and physical health (James 1:2-4, 3:17).
- Setting clear boundaries for yourself and in your relationships and service areas, to reduce the chances of people or situations violating your peace or putting you to avoidable tests.
- Letting higher power, the Holy Spirit of truth, that works righteously in us all the time and in all circumstances (John 16:13 and Philippians 2:13) react for you when in challenging situations and when people provoke you to wrath.

In summary, these definitions characterize peace of mind as a positive and healthy state fostered by the influence of the Holy Spirit within us. It is a condition that individuals can experience, allowing them to live and flourish in harmony with themselves and others.

Peace, scripturally is both the nature of God (Ephesians 2:14) and a gift from God (John 14:27) which transcends all human wisdom, understanding and circumstances, allowing us to always live in a state of quietness and tranquillity even in our troubled, changing and unpredictable world.

—-Peace as God's gift:

"I am leaving you with a gift—peace of mind and heart. And the peace I give is a gift the world cannot give. So don't be troubled or afraid." (John 14:27 NLT).

—-God as Peace by Nature:

"For He Himself is our peace, who has made both one, and has broken down the middle wall of separation," (Ephesians 2:14 NKJV).

THREE-WAY PEACE CONCEPT

Describes the three, relationship peace players. The parts don't have equal weighting. God has the greatest weighting, followed by you and then others. Whereas God can stand alone in this relationship, neither you alone, nor you with others can stand without God.

To have peace, therefore, you MUST connect with God who himself is peace and who gives himself (peace) to us so that our peace within us and with others is guaranteed by the grace He gives.

The relationship among the three, that guarantees you PEACE is illustrated below:

YOU:

- Relate well and do (good) to others as you would like them to do to you.
- Let God the holy spirit rule your life and guide all your ways & actions.

OTHERS (persons, situations)

- Enjoy peace and be grateful when others work for your peace.
- Respond with attitude of hope, love and faith when others fall short or work contrary to your peace and situations do not meet your expectations.

GOD

- The Creator of you and others.
- The author and ultimate guarantor of this peace.
- He Himself is Peace and He gives Himself
- Know Him and know peace

This peace is often characterised by:

ITS INNER FOUNDATION - marked by being rooted in our hearts (Philippians 4:7) and our minds.

CEDING CONTROL TO THE HOLY SPIRIT:

- Releasing Control - casting all your cares, weights, loads, worries and thoughts that bring you doubts and fear on the Lord (1 Peter 5:7; Matthew 11:28-30).
- Letting the Holy Spirit control how you live and react to things which is a sure way to guarantee peace in all circumstances (Galatians 5:22).

SANCTIFIED LIFE

- That models the holy and peaceful nature of God (1 Thessalonians 5:23 NLT)

- That's steady and dependable in all circumstances (Psalm 119:165)

THE GOOD OF ALL WHO SEEK IT

- Harmonious Living by intention (Hebrew 12:14; Romans 14:19; 1 Peter 3:11)
- Seed of Justice by peaceful acts (James 3:18) "Those who make peace sow the seeds of justice by their peaceful acts."

FAITH IN GOD - The more we trust God the more inner peace we have, guaranteed by God Himself, the giver and author of peace (Romans 5:1)

ORDER & CLARITY - Respecting the order established by God, our creator in the structure, service and Governance of families, marriages and even the church and society is the foundation for peace in our world (1Timothy 3:1-13; 1 Corinthians 14:33)

WISDOM & DISCERNMENT in dealing with people (James 3:17)

RESTFUL PHYSICAL STATE - Good sleep and sense of safety (Psalm 4:8)

To know God is to know peace and to have God is to have peace.

"The humbler and more obedient to God a man is, the wiser and at peace he will be in all that he does." — Thomas à Kempis

It's my utmost desire to pass this inspired message about peace, as both God himself by nature, and God's gracious gift to man, which we can harness with intentionality, by yielding to both the gift and the giver, whose empowering influence in our lives (Galatians 5:23 NLT) helps us to lead quiet, healthy and fulfilled life in our families, places of service and in our relationships with both God and man.

"Now may the Lord of peace Himself grant you His peace (the peace of His kingdom) at all times and in all ways [under all circumstances and conditions, whatever comes]. The Lord [be] with you all." (2 Thessalonians 3:16 AMPC)

The next chapter gives insight into experiences that could underpin or test our life of tranquillity and some background to multidimensional peace.

Chapter 2
THE BACKGROUND AND THE CHOICES

"You have everything you need for complete peace and total happiness right now." — Wayne W. Dyer

As a young family in our early years in United Kingdom, during family holidays, we had wonderful moments. I recall a particular holiday period, which we eventually spent at a beachside Caravan in Great Yarmouth, Norfolk, UK. While booking the caravan holiday, I had a profoundly tempting urge to go for an expensive caravan and spend beyond our means. My wife disagreed and we eventually settled for a small but neat and affordable one. There was a particular luxurious and spacious one we both liked but we couldn't afford it without significant financial stress. Common sense and wisdom prevailed. Due to my wife's intervention, we selected what was within our budget at the time and saved ourselves worries that could have resulted from debt. From our small caravan, we enjoyed a splendid beach holiday filled with fun, made possible by reason, intentional planning and choices that were driven by what mattered most to us - peace of mind. The outcome could have differed if we had chosen a different path. Had we chosen immediate gratification and spent outside our budget, it could have left us in debt, possibly cause us spousal friction or family difficulties and steal our peace. For holidaymakers who spent beyond their budget, their time away might have been affected by concerns about debts and potential disagreements over financial matters, or misunderstandings about other minor issues when the underlying cause could be financial constraints.

In our own situation, we chose peace by spending within our income, ignoring frivolities and being intentional with our decisions, spending, and actions.

This agrees with John Denver's expression that ***"Peace is a conscious choice."***

John Denver's wisdom suggests that while external factors can be important determiners of peace, our conscious choices and decisions are essential in cultivating a peaceful state of mind and contributing to peaceful relationships, despite the challenges and temptations we face. This also agrees with the saying that as one makes his bed, so does one lie on it.

Factors that disrupt peace can range from minor incidents, such as arguments over missed calls or appointments, to personal concerns like the fear of aging. Even before considering significant adversities such as health issues, major losses, betrayals, mistrust, infidelity, or financial difficulties, the list of potential threats to peace is extensive. It could be an internal conflict about your identity or unnecessary concern about others' opinions, including about how you were addressed, the tone, or the words used. It could also be self-sabotaging comparison of your possessions, relationships, progress or accomplishments with others', causing you avoidable stress and anxiety.

During a small group breakout session on marriage and family at their convention meeting in London at Good News Church in 2012, Apostle George Amadi and Pastor Chika Amadi, both of whom are practising barristers, accomplished ministers of the Gospel and mentors, discussed the impact of unhealthy comparison lifestyle on peace among young families. Top on their list was a troubling trend of conflicts and disharmony within some young families and couples under 5 years in marital relationships, due to their attitude of destructively comparing themselves, their journeys and achievements with those of seasoned couples in decades old relationships who have longer history of deepened love and affection, physical and emotional intimacy, built-up trust, loyalty, and joint prosperity resulting from shared milestones and victories over challenges and adversities. A good number of the affected young families reportedly ended up bereft of peace in separated or divorced state. For most of the attending young couples and families, including mine, it was distilled wisdom that would inspire us to live empowered family life in the UK.

A few years later, in 2015 during a church service I attended, the pastor of the church delivered a comparable message to a similar audience. The message was about the same comparison lifestyle. The impact on family peace from this plague and its negative consequences on spouses and their children was addressed, with a view to fostering peace and unity and preventing loss of family through separation and divorce. I recall an unsettling experience involving a young couple in their early years of marriage. They frequently quarrelled due to issues related to comparing the wife's family with others, and her dissatisfaction with her husband not meeting her expectations, including her desire for a four-wheel-drive vehicle. These unmet aspirations were driven by the pressure to maintain a certain lifestyle. Despite repeated peace and reconciliation efforts, the couple ultimately divorced. This case highlights the detrimental impact that external influences can have on personal peace and relationships. There are many, similar stories: individuals, families and people in relationships losing their peace over frivolities and marriages falling apart over mundane considerations that should not matter.

The list of peace disruptors is not exhaustive and includes worries, both big and small, over:

- Relationship difficulties with friends, family members or work colleagues.
- Conflict situations, arguments or misunderstandings.
- Challenges with planning events like birthdays, weddings or transitions like buying a house
- Missed appointments, missed deadlines, unmet targets, and backlog of unsorted tasks, even at work.
- A lack of response when expecting communication, or frequent talking when preferring quietness in relationships.
- Debt, utility bills or concerns about financial security.
- Situations involving losses and setbacks, including unsuccessful interviews, failed examinations, and driving tests.
- Work-related pressure, about job and about unemployment, or retirement
- Own health or about the health of family members

Uncontrolled mind can worry about just anything. It could concern internal, yet avoidable, family disputes regarding who is considered the favoured child or issues related to possessions or finances that strain sibling relationships. Stories of family members exiting family fora because of this and other personal and family misunderstandings abound. The list gets even funnier. A man expressed concern about losing his peace when people don't respond quickly to his WhatsApp posts. His was so bad and disabling that it affected his perception of his close friends in the forum - who he believes should be able to comment on his posts - and do so quickly. To "protect his mental health", he decided to stop making posts requiring responses from others.

No age is spared disabling worries that deprive us of our peace. As a secondary school student whose parents were teachers with modest incomes, I remember the pressure during my teenage years to keep up with a close friend from a wealthy background who was always attired in the latest fashion. The fact that my family's expenditures were meticulously planned to align with a pre-determined budget made it impractical and unsustainable for me to attempt to achieve and maintain my friend's lifestyle.

Interestingly, whenever I was about to match his most recent purchase of clothing, he would acquire two or more new items. This left me often troubled and stole my peace until words from my discerning parents gave me behaviour and life-changing insight about a promising future that awaits any focused person of my age then, what mattered most and where my focus should be. This was a turning point in my life. I focused on my academic activities and restored my peace of mind, although it was difficult and required some distance from my innocent friend who was living his usual life. This focus allowed me to succeed in a science school entrance examination, leading to an academic path toward the University.

While sin and transgression are considered affronts to both God and peace, as will be discussed in subsequent chapters, many experiences that disrupt our peace involve behaviours, attitudes, or habits that are not sinful but still breach our boundaries. Protecting one's peace therefore involves establishing boundaries and making decisions that safeguard one's mental, emotional, and spiritual well-being.

Protecting or achieving your inner peace may at times require setting limits and making righteous decisions that, while potentially disappointing to others, are essential for healing your soul, making you more efficient in service and promoting your overall well-being.

During the Easter Saturday Evangelistic outreach on April 2025, organized by my local church, City of David Canterbury and other churches, where I was one of the organisers, a guest speaker cancelled hours before the event due to a scheduling conflict with another program at his church. Despite his initial agreement to attend both events, out of his zeal for the gospel, he ultimately prioritized practical considerations. Despite cancelling with demonstrable regrets and disappointment in his message, with passionate and prophetic prayer **"that all would go well"** for us during the outreach regardless of his absence, I was disappointed by that decision because of how much I valued his participation, until the Holy Spirit whispered to me **"he did it for his peace"** and reminded me the title of my book on peace. I gladly responded and thanked him for getting back to me and for his prayers.

To demonstrate that nothing is unforeseen by God and that the occurrence was part of His plan, God provided another evangelist who subsequently filled this gap in the program of the event, much to the astonishment of myself and other event planners aware of this development. It was another opportunity to re-learn the peace that goes with insightful understanding of Romans 8:28 which writes:

"And we know that God causes everything to work together for the good of those who love God and are called according to his purpose for them."

Reminiscing on Charles R. Swindoll's ***"life is 10% versus 90%"*** quote, the above experience should remind us that in all circumstances, when we feel disappointed with people's actions and where the reality on ground does not match our expectations, we should endeavour to avoid self-focused tendency, embrace empowering, altruistic mindset that treats others with care and empathy, and respond with calm, gratitude, supplication and prayer for God's will upon which our peace is centred, according to the wisdom of Philippians 4:6-7.

Whether it is the holiday experience, the spousal lifestyle comparison or other situations that tested personal and ministerial priorities, the focus was on maintaining peace, guided by discernment and self-control with deliberate and inspired thoughtful decisions.

Peace is an essential requirement for man to live a healthy and fulfilled life. It provides an account of life from an experiential perspective, highlighting its lived and enjoyed aspects. Peace is beyond theory; it is practical, better experienced than imagined and peace can be shared. To understand true peace, you must experience it. Words that portray peace include order, calmness, quietude, tranquillity, stillness, restfulness and many more.

Life is a journey inevitably replete with shared experiences that challenge our peace. A truly healthy life is one that we live in the glory of quietness on all sides as much as depends on us, and as much as we can leverage the gift of peace from our maker in our lived and shared life experiences.

Since peace cannot be found by avoiding life's challenges, the next chapter offers a scriptural example of maintaining peace amid difficulties, highlighting the principle of multidimensional peace.

Chapter 3

QUIET IN STERN; CALM IN STORM

"When you go through deep waters, I will be with you. When you go through rivers of difficulty, you will not drown. When you walk through the fire of oppression, you will not be burned up; the flames will not consume you."
(Isaiah 43:2 NLT)

Challenges are unavoidable as long as the earth exists. A life devoid of challenges, difficulties, and trials is indicative of a world lacking tests and advancements. Peace does not imply the absence of conflicts, nor do difficulties signify the absence or cessation of peace.

Sheila Walsh writes: ***"Peace is not the absence of trouble, but the presence of Christ."***

And the story of Jesus in the stern in the stormy Sea of Galilee confirms it.

THE SEA OF GALILEA STORM: Jesus in the Stern, Calm in the Storm

"On that same day [when] evening had come, He (Jesus) said to them, Let us go over to the other side [of the lake]. And leaving the throng, they took Him with them, [just] as He was, in the boat [in which He was sitting]. And other boats were with Him. And a FURIOUS STORM of wind [of hurricane proportions] arose, and the waves kept beating into the boat, so that it was already becoming filled. But He [Himself] was IN THE STERN [of the boat], asleep on the [leather] cushion; and they awoke Him and said to Him, Master, do You not care that we are perishing? And He arose and rebuked the wind and said to the sea, Hush now! Be still (muzzled)! And the wind ceased (sank to rest as if exhausted by its beating) and there was [immediately] a great calm (a perfect peacefulness). He said to them, Why are you so timid and fearful? How is it that you have no faith (no firmly relying trust)? And they were filled with great awe and feared exceedingly and said one to another, Who then is this, that even wind and sea obey Him?" (Mark 4:35-41 AMPC).

The Sea of Galilee is well known for its violent storms. As the storm caused the disciples to worry for their lives and safety, Jesus, awakened from sleep in the stern, instructed the storm to stop, and with the words "Peace, be still," he calmed the water.

The writer of the Gospel, Mark, tells us that the violent stormy wind "ceased" and there was a great calm.

Remember the Characters at play here:

- Jesus – the originator of the journey.
- His Disciples – the obedient followers.

Remember the natural elements involved:

- Sea of water.
- The Wind.

Then observe the driver of the journey and the order of events:

- Jesus called and took the disciples on this journey, just like He takes us in our journeys in this life.
- The disciples honoured and obeyed their all-knowing master, the same way we are encouraged and commanded to obey God for Him to manifest Himself to us (John 14:15-21, 27).
- Jesus went to sleep in the STERN (rearmost part of the boat or ship) as they sailed in the sea, a period of God's rest and quietness, comparable in our lives to times when God may seem silent or distant to us.
- Mid-way in the journey (Jesus in the Stern asleep), the dangerous windstorm arose, leaving Christ's disciples afraid for their lives, just as we often panic when challenges come and answers to our prayers seem delayed.

And the interplay of natural elements with Christ, speaks:

- The boisterous wind triggered the sea wave that "beat into the boat" causing it to begin to fill.
- While the boat was beginning to fill with water, Jesus rebuked the wind and not the water.
- To the Wind Christ gave a rebuke and to the Sea of water, He gave three-worded soothing balm "peace be still."

This story clearly exemplifies:

- The humanity of Christ: That Christ experienced human conditions such as fatigue and the need for rest, demonstrating that a relationship with Christ does not exempt one from challenges and hardships. But sanctified relationship guarantees holy spirit and the blessing of peace (Galatians 5:22-23).
- The cost and rewards of discipleship - highlighting the trials faced by His disciples due to their obedience, along with the victory and peace promised by His presence, for those who follow His will.
- The spoken word that possesses significant power—its transformative nature being able to move mountains, alter destinies, and revive the deceased. This power is consistent through time—yesterday, today, and in the future—and provides peace and solace during times of difficulty.
- The power of His presence - that guaranteed peace and safety for His disciples in difficulties, which is also available to us as children of timeless, changeless, and ever-present God in our times of need.
- Strength in weakness - Christ's strength being perfected in our weakest moments (2 Corinthians 12:9) just as His was perfected for the disciples' weakest moment in the storm.
- The peace of God that surpasses all human understanding that can be attained through seeking Him in faith, applying wisdom and discernment as demonstrated by the disciples during their challenging times in that storm on the Sea of Galilee.

PEACE IN THAT STORM: CHRIST AN EXAMPLE

This remarkable story tells of:

- Christ asleep in the STERN
- Christ stilling the boisterous STORM

Although Christ was in the stern of the ship, He was peacefully asleep on a pillow.

THE STERN AND ITS SIGNIFICANCE

The stern is recognised as the rearmost section of a ship. It is considered vulnerable due to its position and the fragility of certain components in some vessels. The contents and vital functions housed within this area, including the steering mechanism, are susceptible to potential damage that can affect the functioning of the ship.

CRIPPLING EFFECT AND ITS FRAGILITY

The stern of a ship contains the rudder and propeller system, which are crucial for controlling the vessel's movement. Damage to the stern can significantly affect the ship's manoeuvrability and its ability to stay on course. A direct hit to the external rudder located at the stern would render the ship *unsteerable*. The stern, typically designed with a lighter and more delicate structure compared to the sides, is also more prone to structural damage.

ANCHOR SYSTEM & REAR LOCATION VULNERABILITY

The stern, recognized as a crucial point for securing the ship to the anchor, is especially vulnerable during berthing and docking procedures. Its exposed rear position in sailing vessels makes it particularly susceptible to attacks by sea pirates and to damage from enemy cannon fire.

Additionally, it is important to note that the noise generated by the stern's propulsion system can significantly impact comfort during sea travel. This noise does not facilitate restful relaxation or quality sleep by any standard.

PEACE IN THE STERNS & STORMS OF OUR LIVES

The stern could disputably but fairly be likened to our spiritual journeys as followers of Christ, where we expect peace through righteous living, yet encounter disruptions from the everyday world and challenges inherent in our callings and vocations. Our storms could easily represent the trials, tests, and tribulations God has allowed us to face as He takes us in our life journeys.

In a critical moment that can pass as the storm of his life, Moses encountered a significant experience with a burning bush. During this event, as described in Exodus 3:4-8, he was able to pause, reflect, turn and listen to a voice that defined his destiny and provided him with instructions for his calling, giving his life purpose and direction. For Stephen, during a life-ending storm of his life, when most carnal men would call down fire to consume their enemies, filled with the peace of the Holy spirit, discernment and inspired heart of love for the salvation of sinners, as he gazed into heaven beholding the glory of God, Stephen, according to Acts 7:59-60 was compassionate enough to pray prayer of forgiveness for his killers:

"And while they were stoning Stephen, he prayed, Lord Jesus, receive *and* accept *and* welcome my spirit! And falling on his knees, he cried out loudly, Lord, fix not this sin upon them [lay

it not to their charge]! And when he had said this, he fell asleep [in death]."

Paul, who was a beneficiary of Stephen's prayer, called by the saving Grace of God (Acts 9:15), would eventually reflect, through writing, Stephen's virtue of love and forgiveness (among others) in his message to the Romans:

"**Beloved, never avenge yourselves, but leave the way open for [God's] wrath; for it is written, Vengeance is Mine, I will repay (requite), says the Lord [20] But if your enemy is hungry, feed him; if he is thirsty, give him drink; for by so doing you will heap burning coals upon his head. Do not let yourself be overcome by evil, but overcome (master) evil with good."** (Romans 12:21 AMPC)

When Paul found peace in Christ, anchored in his divine vocation, he, through the grace of God and the wisdom acquired from revelation, was insightful enough to proclaim in Acts 14:22: "... we must through many tribulations enter the kingdom of God" and in the face of many tribulations and unbearable persecution Paul, steadfast in faith could say:

"We are pressed on every side by troubles, but we are not crushed. We are perplexed, but not driven to despair. We are hunted down, but never abandoned by God. We get knocked down, but we are not destroyed. Through suffering, our bodies continue to share in the death of Jesus so that the life of Jesus may also be seen in our bodies. Yes, we live under constant danger of death because we serve Jesus, so that the life of Jesus will be evident in our dying bodies. [1]So we live in the face of death, but this has resulted in eternal life for you. But we continue to preach because we have the same kind of faith the psalmist had when he said, "I believed in God, so I spoke." We know that God, who raised the Lord Jesus, will also raise us

with Jesus and present us to himself together with you. All of this is for your benefit. And as God's grace reaches more and more people, there will be great thanksgiving, and God will receive more and more glory." (2 Corinthians 4:8-15)

And when they though Paul was to give up due to unbearable storm, he remained faithful to his calling, resolute in his kingdom conviction, that he could, to the Church in Phillipi, say:

"I don't mean to say that I have already achieved these things or that I have already reached perfection. But I press on to possess that perfection for which Christ Jesus first possessed me. No, dear brothers and sisters, I have not achieved it, but I focus on this one thing: Forgetting the past and looking forward to what lies ahead, I press on to reach the end of the race and receive the heavenly prize for which God, through Christ Jesus, is calling us." (Philippians 3:12-14 NLT)

When we experience storms in our lives, what is our first reaction? Who do we run to first and how do we respond, for our peace? Do we seek the face of God for clarity before reacting with discernment or do we respond with impulsive confusion that makes the matter worse and then run to God as a last resort when our boat is on the brink of capsizing? How can we model the kind of Peace Christ had in the stern despite the short-comings of that environment, and how can we respond to silent-appearing Christ when in the storms of our lives (in our marriages, businesses, relationships and other life experiences)? Will you, like in the case of the disciples, be asked why are you so fearful and how is it that you have no faith (to trust God for help in your marriage, in the challenges with your job or raising of your children, in ungodly addictive behaviour, your struggle with finance, anger or unforgiveness, or your struggle with getting over that betrayal or disappointing human experience)?

It's important to note that in the situation at the Sea of Galilea, it was not their anxiety over the threat of the storm or their fear of it that led Jesus to remark that they had **no faith**. A small boat in a large storm can be an unsettling situation, and initial fear is understandable. How the disciples responded to the fear particularly while they had Christ next door (in the stern) was what mattered.

Jesus could say they had **no faith** because they did not react as those who believed His word. They each heard Jesus say, **"Let us go over to the other side of the lake"** (Mark 4:35). His nature, His words and their knowledge and witness of what He had done in the past should be enough to reassure them of a safe arrival. The disciples had the option to trust in that assurance; however, their panic and reaction indicate they did not. In this regard, they displayed a lack of faith. Jesus could further confirm their lack of faith, as evidenced by their subsequent actions. When they later woke Him, they sceptically questioned His concern for them by asking, "Do you not care that we are perishing?" (Mark 4:38)

What was an opportunity for the disciples to leverage their knowledge of Christ and His power turned into dead faith experience with risk of drowning in the sea. The disciples should (from their experience and understanding of the Lord and His mission on earth as our Messiah) have known that God would not allow His son to perish in a boat crossing the Sea of Galilee. Jesus could further say they had **no faith** because they forgot this big picture and risked perishing if not for Christ's intervention, for lack of application of this knowledge. No wonder Hosea writes:

"My people are destroyed for lack of knowledge. Because you have rejected knowledge, I also will reject you from being priest for Me; Because you have forgotten the law of your God, I also will forget your children." (Hosea 4:6).

When we encounter difficulties and fail to trust in God's guidance, seeking human solutions in panic and neglecting His promises until we face desperate situations, we resemble the disciples on the Sea of Galilee, we lose our peace and miss His plans and purposes for us.

When we think Jesus doesn't care about us, it shows we have **no faith**, because we don't believe the truth about Christ. It takes great faith to trust the sleeping Jesus, to know that He cares and works for us even when it does not *seem* like it. But this is the kind of trust God wants to build in us. Of all people, Jesus' own disciples should have had faith. Would Jesus put the same question to us?

The story of Elijah and his flight from Jezebel is another instructive experience.

Elijah was a man whom God used to do many mighty things. However, when word reached him that Jezebel had threatened his life, instead of trusting in the Lord who, not long ago gave him victory over 450 prophets of Ball, he ran (1 Kings chapter 19). Elijah, showing, the frail, instead of the faith side of his humanity, prayed despondently to the LORD and in effect complained about how he was being treated: **"He replied, 'I have been very zealous for the LORD God Almighty. The Israelites have rejected your covenant, torn down your altars, and put your prophets to death with the sword. I am the only one left, and now they are trying to kill me too."** (1 Kings 19:10)

The LORD'S answer to Elijah is soul-searching: **"The Lord said, 'Go out and stand on the mountain in the presence of the Lord, for the Lord is about to pass by.' Then a great and powerful wind tore the mountains apart and shattered the rocks before the Lord, but the Lord was not in the wind. After the wind there was an earthquake, but the Lord was not in the earthquake.**

After the earthquake came a fire, but the Lord was not in the fire. And after the fire came a gentle whisper" (1 Kings 19:11-12).

We see in this passage of Scripture that what Elijah thought, was not true. Elijah thought God was silent and that he was the only one left. God was not only "not silent," but He had a massive army waiting in the wings so that Elijah was not alone: **"Yet I reserve seven thousand in Israel—all whose knees have not bowed down to Baal and whose mouths have not kissed him"** (1 Kings 19:18). God showed up to help Prophet Elijah in his lowest moment of need and human frailty, a pivotal experience that also re-defined his ministry (read 1 Kings 18 and 19).

In our walk as believers, we lose our peace when it may seem that God is silent, but God is never silent. God is always available; in fact, He is our ever-present help particularly in our times of need (Hebrews 4:16). What looks like silence and divine inactivity or passivity to us is God allowing us the opportunity to exercise and grow in our power of belief, to listen to "the still small voice" and to see and leverage the provisions that He has made for us by faith.

All we need at this point is to be discerning and still, and to be obedient and patient, wait for the manifestation of God's purpose after we've exercised our living faith. The psalmist has this well captured:

"God is our refuge and strength, a very present help in trouble... Be still, and know that I am God; I will be exalted among the nations, I will be exalted in the earth!" (Psalm 46:1, 10).

And James 1:2-4 captures the outcome and what our manner of waiting should be:

"Dear brothers and sisters, when troubles of any kind come your way, consider it an opportunity for great joy. For you know

that when your faith is tested, your endurance has a chance to grow. So let it grow, for when your endurance is fully developed, you will be perfect and complete, needing nothing." (James 1:2-4)

The scripture is clear that we matter to God, who is interested in us, taking notice of every area of our lives, including the very hairs on our heads which are numbered by Him (Matthew 10:30). There are times however, when God allows trials in our lives, with intent to edify us, meaning we are particularly expected to follow divine principles and work in sanctified obedience for God to give us further insights, as growth often comes through experience that comes from applying what we learn.

Our peace stems from a practical understanding and appreciation that in our thoughts and responses to events, challenges, and trials, the wisdom of God is complex for the carnal individual to comprehend, and His ways differ from ours.

"'For my thoughts are not your thoughts, neither are your ways my ways,' declares the Lord. 'As the heavens are higher than the earth, so are my ways higher than your ways and my thoughts than your thoughts. As the rain and the snow come down from heaven, and do not return to it without watering the earth and making it bud and flourish, so that it yields seed for the sower and bread for the eater, so is my word that goes out from my mouth: It will not return to me empty, but will accomplish what I desire and achieve the purpose for which I sent it.'" (Isaiah 55:8-11)

Therefore, when God seems silent to us, it may suggest that we have stopped listening to His voice; that we have allowed the cares of this world to plug our spiritual ears, or we have neglected His word. God may today not speak to you in pillars of cloud, wind, wave of the sea or the fire and smoke of Mount Sinai, but

His Spirit speaks to us through the Word of God in which we have the "words of life and peace."

Prophet Isaiah reminds us His word:

"When you pass through the waters, I will be with you; and when you pass through the rivers, they will not sweep over you" (Isaiah 43:2)

The experience of the disciples where Peter walked on the water until he began to sink when he took his focus off Jesus, is another demonstration that Jesus always comes to us in the storms of life (Read Matthew 14, please). Jesus came to His rescue with insightful and corrective remark about the cause of His sinking – doubt. The Lord may not come at the time we think He should come, because He knows when we need Him the most. Jesus (in the case of Peter walking on water) had waited until their boat was as far from land as possible, when all their hope was gone. In essence, Jesus was testing the disciples' faith, and this meant removing every opportunity to rely on humans. What was the purpose of Jesus walking on water? To show His disciples that the very thing they feared, the raging, seething sea, was merely a set of steps for the Lord to come to them. Often, we fear the difficult experiences of life such as job losses, betrayals, failures, financial hardships and trials in our families and Ministries only to discover that these experiences may have been allowed by divinity to take us to a wealthier place and place of His purpose, or to bring us closer to Jesus.

Turning our attention again to the stern of the boat: notwithstanding the issues, challenges and vulnerabilities of this section, Jesus remained rested and at peace in the stern.

Consider all the concerns that could have potentially caused Jesus to be restless, anxious, panicked, and awake:

- The disturbance.
- The open space and its susceptibility to attack.
- The structural weakness of the stern.
- The potential for malfunction within the engine and propeller system.
- The responsibilities of the Master's ministry and demanding schedules.

Consider all potential worries that could have stolen Christ's peace:

- He could have worried about the Scribes, the Pharisees and the Sadducees with whom he often had confrontations, or the religious and political leaders who always plotted against Him. This compares to the same way you worry about people like this who you should not be worried about and whose behaviour should stir you to good works.
- He could have been concerned about the large crowds that frequently gather around him (Matthew 9:36) with their numerous needs, like how we sometimes struggle to set appropriate boundaries and address the issues of our family members and acquaintances despite having limited resources.
- He could worry about his chosen disciples and their ability to meet expectations and be a true light to the world, or their fate after His departure.

You can liken this to the way you overly worry about your children or those who are under your tutelage as though you want to live their lives for them or do their work for them to perfection, and this takes toll on your mental peace.

He could also worry about His future plans for the Church, knowing the difficult hours ahead and what His destiny would be. He could worry about what would be said of Him when Peter denies Him and Judas finally betrays Him for thirty pieces of silver.

And He could even more dejectedly worry about:

- His home country where He did not do many mighty works because of their unbelief (Matthew 13:58)
- His immediate family who thought He was crazy (Mark 3:21) and
- His own brothers who didn't believe in Him (John 7:5)

With all these potentially depressing concerns to worry about, Jesus wasn't worried. He instead slept in a rocking boat, well rested and unperturbed by the internal and external noises. And the Lord's rest and sleep were not just only those of tiredness: they were driven by living faith regardless of what was happening around Him

And they awoke Him…

The wind didn't wake Him, the noisy stern and its propeller system didn't wake Him, and water splashing over the boat didn't wake Him. But at the cry of His disciples, He was instantly awoken. Jesus is like the mother who sleeps through all kinds of unpleasant noise, but at the slightest noise from her little baby, she instantly awakes. The rest was authentic and the sleep deep.

And as the Psalmist writes, what He has. He also gives to those who have confident trust in Him:

"**In peace I will both lie down and sleep, for You, Lord, alone make me dwell in safety and confident trust**." (Psalm 4:8 AMPC)

AWAKEN TO THE RAVAGING STORM...

Jesus did not panic. He knew that He was in His Father's will and that no matter what else happened around Him, His Father's will would still be fulfilled in Him. With discernment, compassion, and confidence in His identity, He commanded the storm to cease immediately.

The very practice of Christ resting and sleeping during a particularly challenging period provides valuable insight into maintaining calm and tranquillity in the middle of crisis. It suggests that one can attain peace amidst turmoil by trusting in a higher authority to manage anxieties and problems, with the confidence that one is walking and acting in accordance with God's will.

We can learn from Jesus. Just as Christ our Master stayed calm and guided his disciples from trouble, we should trust the Lord's guidance to stay peaceful in difficult times instead of panicking without trust in His ability to save us.

"Trust in the Lord with all your heart. And lean not on your own understanding; In all your ways acknowledge Him, And He shall direct your path." (Proverbs 3:5-6).

CHRIST'S HUMANITY IN THE STORM – A LESSON

After addressing a large gathering, Christ needed to cross to the other side. Simultaneously, He required physical rest for His body. This scenario highlights two crucial aspects of Christ's humanity: His need for rest and solitude, and His ability to sleep soundly despite the tumultuous conditions. While scripture indicates that the Lord neither slumbers nor sleeps (Psalm 121:4), Jesus, in His human form, slept in the boat. Even amidst fatigue and the storm, Jesus remained calm and undisturbed, exemplifying an absence of worry or stress in crisis.

The fact that Jesus, our Creator and Master, experienced the storm despite His righteous and holy nature serves as an important lesson for us. It highlights that:

We are not exempt from trials and tests.

Our righteousness does not shield us from experiencing life's challenges even though it guarantees us outcome that's consistent with God's will if we work in obedience.

If therefore our sinless Master faced such difficulties, we, as imperfect beings, should also anticipate encountering similar situations.

"A disciple is not above his teacher, nor a servant above his master." (Matthew 10:24 NKJV)

This indicates that challenges are inevitable part of life, as affirmed by the teachings and reflected in the Gospel of John.

"I have told you all this so that you may have peace in me. Here on earth you will have many trials and sorrows. But take heart, because I have overcome the world." (John 16:33 NLT)

But here is our consolation:

In a similar manner, just as Christ prevailed over the storm, we too can surmount life's challenges by harnessing His power that operates within us (Ephesians 3:20 & Philippians 2:13), if we remain in Him (John 15:1-7). Consequently, we should be assured that storms, temptations, and trials are all under the sovereign control of our Creator, which is why Apostle Paul could write as follows:

"No temptation [regardless of its source] has overtaken or enticed you that is not common to human experience [nor is any temptation unusual or beyond human resistance]; but God is faithful [to His word—He is compassionate and trustworthy], and He will not let you be tempted beyond your ability [to resist], but along with the temptation He [has in the past and is now and] will [always] provide the way out as well, so that you will be able to endure it [without yielding, and will overcome temptation with joy]." (1 Corinthians 10:13 AMP)

CHRIST REBUKING THE WIND: A LESSON IN PEACE AND DISCERNMENT

Discernment is essential for maintaining a peaceful life, and it represents a divine call for intercession. This role is not intended for fault-finding or seeking revenge, but rather for serving one another with compassion and love. During storms discernment enables you to know who or what your real enemy is so that you can deal with it and direct your therapy or battle to the appropriate quarter. Christ authored and leveraged this principle.

Individuals such as your brother, sister, friend, and colleague at work are not inherently adversaries. While challenges may arise in relationships and external influences can disrupt your peace and harmony with others, it is important to recognize that scripture identifies our common adversary as the devil.

Jesus exemplifies discernment, as demonstrated in the scenario where He recognized Satan as the adversary when Peter, in Matthew 16:22-23, took Him aside and rebuked Him for foretelling His death and expressing His willingness to submit Himself to crucifixion.

Jesus' reaction was instant and apt:

"But He turned and said to Peter, "Get behind Me, Satan! You are an offense to Me, for you are not mindful of the things of God, but the things of men." (Matthew 16:23 NKJV).

Get behind Me, Satan! This was a forceful and yet appropriate rebuke from Jesus. Though a moment earlier, Peter spoke as a messenger of God, in this scenario, he spoke as a messenger of **Satan**. Jesus was discerning and knew there was a satanic purpose in Peter discouraging Him from His ministry on the cross, and Jesus would not allow that purpose to succeed. It is evident that Peter was unaware of his role as an agent of Satan in this context, just as he was previously unaware that he had been speaking on behalf of God when he rightly identified Jesus as The Christ, the Son of the living God (Matthew 16:16). It is often much easier to be a tool of God for peace or of the devil against peace than we want to believe.

Having learnt a lesson in discernment, Apostle Peter writes:

"Stay alert! Watch out for your great enemy, the devil. He prowls around like a roaring lion, looking for someone to devour. Stand firm against him and be strong in your faith. Remember that your family of believers all over the world is going through the same kind of suffering you are." (1 Peter 5:8-9 NLT)

This scripture suggests to us that everyone is a target and needs help in conflict situation and in moments of hostilities which are clearly the handiwork of our adversary, the devil. Thus, in the Sea of Galilee situation, we can clearly identify the target and the adversary.

Therefore, Jesus delivered a stern and forceful command to the WIND to cease. He then addressed the SEA, saying, "Peace, be still!"

This tells us the wind, not the water, is the enemy. The turbulent sea appeared to be at the mercy of the wind, and the violent waves subsided immediately when the stormy wind was rebuked into stillness. Following this, the master commanded the sea water, saying, "Peace, be still."

Therefore, when a family member, friend, or colleague is behaving inappropriately or in a manner that disrupts your peace, whether at home, in the workplace, or elsewhere, it is important to pause and assess the situation. Determine if there may be external influences, personal challenges or trials affecting their behaviour. Understanding this will equip you with the appropriate knowledge on how to address the issue effectively. In some situation, what such person needs may be you're your prayer, empathy or constructive feedback and truth (Ephesians 4:15, 25).

Life is both physical and spiritual and a win for peace in the spiritual world, will guarantee us peace in the physical world.

For this reason, Paul, to the Ephesian Christians writes:

"Put on all of God's armour so that you will be able to stand firm against all strategies of the devil. For we are not fighting against flesh-and-blood enemies, but against evil rulers and authorities of the unseen world, against mighty powers in this dark world, and against evil spirits in the heavenly places. Therefore, put on every piece of God's armour so you will be able to resist the enemy in the time of evil. Then after the battle you will still be standing firm." (Ephesian 6:11-13 NLT).

Often, we ignorantly fight human agents and inadvertently target victims instead of the actual culprits, or involve ourselves in unnecessary disputes in relationships, marriages, churches, workplaces and in families over rights, positions, and trivial matters, enslave ourselves in perpetual conflicts and deny ourselves peace. It is therefore our responsibility to act with discernment and serve one another with love. This approach can effectively address conflicts, hostility, and the pursuit of power and influence over others.

On the power of love and peace, Jimi Hendrix writes: ***"When the power of love overcomes the love of power, the world will know peace."***

WE ARE TO ACT AS DISCIPLES OF PEACE

"When He was reviled and insulted, He did not revile or offer insult in return; [when] He was abused and suffered, He made no threats [of vengeance]; but he trusted [Himself and everything] to Him Who judges fairly." (1 Peter 2: 23 AMPC).

Christ Himself is both Peace (Ephesians 2:14) and giver of Peace (John 14:27), meaning that as faithful disciples (Mark 8:34) we are called to be what He is - peace, and take what He has freely given to us - peace.

As disciples of peace, we must reflect the nature and character of Jesus. Therefore, it is essential for us to be advocates of peace, emulating the teachings of Christ, who embodies love and bestows peace upon us. During Sermon on the Mount, our Saviour commanded us to reflect His nature in Pursuit of virtues that make for peace, the greatest of which is love.

Here is Matthew's account of our Lord's teaching:

"But I say, love your enemies! Pray for those who persecute you! In that way, you will be acting as true children of your Father in heaven. For he gives his sunlight to both the evil and the good, and he sends rain on the just and the unjust alike...you are to be perfect, even as your Father in heaven is perfect." (Matthew 5: 44-45, 48 NLT)

This describes love manifesting its pure attributes, the core of which is peace.

According to Galatians 5:22-23, the spirit produces peace. Therefore, fostering peaceful relationships with others reflects the compassionate nature of your father, who embodies peace himself.

When situations arise that endanger our peace, we are not expected to succumb or surrender. Instead, we are encouraged to address those circumstances in accordance with our obedience to Christ, as Paul articulates:

"We can demolish every deceptive fantasy that opposes God and break through every arrogant attitude (including those opposed to PEACE) that is raised up in defiance of the true knowledge of God. We capture, like prisoners of war, every thought (including thought of CONFLICTS) and insist that it bow in obedience to the Anointed One." (2 Corinthians 10:5 TPT).

Exactly what David did in his trying times when his rebellious son, Absalom led a failed attempt to dethrone him (David) and simultaneously, a man called Shimea threatened David's peace and dignity with insults and mockery.

David's reaction was apt, humbling and empowering.

Here is account of this in 2 Samuel 16:

"As King David came to Bahurim, a man came out of the village cursing them. It was Shimei son of Gera, from the same clan as Saul's family. He threw stones at the king and the king's officers and all the mighty warriors who surrounded him. "Get out of here, you murderer, you scoundrel!" he shouted at David. "The Lord is paying you back for all the bloodshed in Saul's clan. You stole his throne, and now the Lord has given it to your son Absalom. At last you will taste some of your own medicine, for you are a murderer!" "Why should this dead dog curse my Lord the king?" Abishai son of Zeruiah demanded. "Let me go over and cut off his head!" "No!" the king said. "Who asked your opinion, you sons of Zeruiah! If the Lord has told him to curse me, who are you to stop him?" Then David said to Abishai and to all his servants, "My own son is trying to kill me. Doesn't this relative of Saul have even more reason to do so? Leave him alone and let him curse, for the Lord has told him to do it. And perhaps the Lord will see that I am being wronged and will bless me because of these curses today." So David and his men continued down the road, and Shimei kept pace with them on a nearby hillside, cursing and throwing stones and dirt at David. The king and all who were with him grew weary along the way, so they rested when they reached the Jordan River." (2 Samuel 16: 5-14 NLT).

Here we see this clearly resentful Shimea, a distant relative of King Saul, insult David for replacing Saul. His behaviour was highly provocative and deeply disrespectful, with the intention of undermining David's remaining honour as he (David) faced the threat of being dethroned by his own son.

This unprovoked action can be compared to a declaration of war. To comprehend meekness and the qualities of a peaceful individual, consider this description of King David, the man who Shimea confronted:

"...he is a brave warrior, a man of war, and has good judgment...and the Lord is with him." (1 Samuel 16:18 NLT)

David could easily instruct one of his mighty men, his army, or his bodyguard to take Shimea's head off, but he didn't. He could use his power as a king to deal with Shimei. He did not run away from the man's disparaging remarks and unpleasant words, and he didn't close his ears to unpleasant and critical remarks.

How did David react?

David was willing to receive messages from God through various sources, including Shimea, who was critical of him. He also stopped his men from harming Shimea. David clearly understood that if he did what was right and please God in that moment of trial, God would take care of the future. Instead of invoking his man-of-war character, David chose meekness with his good and inspired judgment side, and responded with Grace.

David, in this context, is an example and description of inward peace experienced by individuals who maintain fellowship with their spiritual beliefs, and who reflect these beliefs in their motives, words, and actions.

In response to David's act of Grace, Shimea became, repentant and pleaded for forgiveness, according to 2 Samuel 19:18-23 NLT)

As the king was about to cross the river, Shimei fell down before him. "My Lord the king, please forgive me," he pleaded. "Forget the terrible thing your servant did when you left Jerusalem. May the king put it out of his mind. I know how much I sinned. That is why I have come here today, the very first

person in all Israel to greet my Lord the king." Then Abishai son of Zeruiah said, "Shimei should die, for he cursed the Lord's anointed king!" "Who asked your opinion, you sons of Zeruiah!" David exclaimed. "Why have you become my adversary today? This is not a day for execution, for today I am once again the king of Israel!" Then, turning to Shimei, David vowed, "Your life will be spared." (2 Samuel 19: 18-23 NLT)

David, through these spirit-inspired acts of kindness, humility, gentleness, love, self-control and ultimately PEACE demonstrated here, forcefully spoke with Paul's message to the Romans: **"Never let evil defeat you, but defeat evil with good."** (Romans 12:21 TPT)

The question is how do you respond to disparaging remarks or behaviour you consider disrespectful from people over whom you have authority?

How do you react when offended, maligned or insulted, especially by people in lower social position than yourself?

Do you react with rage or grace?

Do you respond with loving or loathing?

As a Leader, how do you treat your critics?

- Do you, unlike King David, use your position to suppress contrary opinions regardless of their worthiness and give platform to your praise singers?
- In your family, establishment or ministry, do you use your power and authority to deny dissenting voices opportunities and reward your favourites or colluding allies with roles, without regard to merit?

No wonder William E. Gladstone again writes: ***"Until the Power of Love replaced the Love of Power, our world will not know the blessings of peace."***

In whatever circumstances we find ourselves, therefore, we're encouraged to respond to adversity or offence with actions that pass peace test in love and revenge, according to Paul's admonition to the Roman Church:

"Never pay back evil with evil. Do things in such a way that everyone can see you are honourable. Do all that you can to live in peace with everyone." (Romans 12:17-18 NLT).

YOUR PEACE IN YOUR HAND

If we are self-aware or perceptive, the peace we seek can be found internally rather than externally.

During his calling by God, Moses, feeling anxious and uncertain, was anticipating solutions from elsewhere. However, the Lord encouragingly inquired what he had in his hand, revealing its invaluable worth (Exodus 4:2). Ultimately, that in his hand, the rod of Moses became a symbol of God's authority, leading to their miraculous deliverance from slavery in Egypt.

God's blessings and peace are not always far off; they can be as near as your knees are to the ground, and as immediate as when your heart and words reach out to Him.

"It shall come to pass That before they call, I will answer; And while they are still speaking, I will hear." (Isaiah 65:24 NKJV).

During the incident on the Sea of Galilee, it seems that the disciples turned to Jesus as a final measure when the storm escalated beyond their capacity to manage either independently or through other means.

It is likely that the disciples exhausted all other options before waking Jesus. When their efforts proved unsuccessful, they decided to wake Him.

"Then He arose and rebuked the wind, and said to the sea, "Peace, be still!" And the wind ceased and there was a great calm. But He said to them, "Why are you so fearful? How is it that you have no faith?" And they feared exceedingly, and said to one another, "Who can this be, that even the wind and the sea obey Him!"" (Mark 4:39-41 NKJV)

How did they overlook using what was readily available?

It is noteworthy and concerning too that despite having our sovereign God, the Creator of the world and all that is in it with them, they seemed unaware of the solution that lay within.

Amidst the noise of the sea waves and the threatening boisterous wind, they became distracted by external factors and overlooked the most important asset within their possession - the Son of God, the creator of the natural elements (the sea, the waves, and the windstorm), who was present in the boat.

In times of crisis, particularly in relationships where peace is threatened, individuals often focus on external distractions and forces that seek to divide them, as well as potential temptations. It is important, however, not to lose sight of the bond of love that initially brought them together. This should always be remembered and prioritized.

"Why are you fearful? How is it that you have no faith?" These rhetorical questions posed by Jesus to His disciples were intended as a rebuttal, emphasizing that His presence in the boat was sufficient to allay their fears. The underlying message was that their focus should have been on Him rather than on their external threats.

The miracle Jesus did over nature here, which shows his demonstration of what God intends for humans of dominion (Genesis 1:25-30), to be and do, should have empowering influence over us, to believe that we can do all things through Christ who strengthens us (Philippians 2:13) if remember and choose WHAT WE HAVE IN OUR HANDS - our gifts and blessings.

- Where do you run to when difficulties that challenge your peace arise in your family and/or relationships?
- Do you first look inside your boat for a solution, or outside at the sea, waves, and storm?
- Do you reflect internally to identify the qualities within you, such as love, peace, patience, kindness, gentleness, self-control and similar virtues, as mentioned in Galatians 5:22-23 and 1 Corinthians 13:4-13 to help you overcome?

Many individuals in difficult relationships often believe that involving a third party will expedite conflict resolution. However, evidence suggests that this approach may not be the most effective. A notable example of successful direct communication is found in the reconciliation meeting between Jacob and Esau, which was achieved through honest and open dialogue (Genesis 33).

The reunion meeting, which facilitated reconciliation between the prodigal son and his father, occurred through a direct conversation. This interaction provided an opportunity to address past issues, restore the son's position within the family, and achieve mutual understanding and peace.

Luke 15:17-24 captures this by saying:

17 "When he came to his senses, he said, 'How many of my
father's hired servants have food to spare, and here I am
starving to death! 18 I will set out and go back to my father and
say to him: Father, I have sinned against heaven and against
you. 19 I am no longer worthy to be called your son; make me
like one of your hired servants.' 20 So he got up and went to his
father.

"But while he was still a long way off, his father saw him and was filled with compassion for him; he ran to his son, threw his arms around him and kissed him.

21 "The son said to him, 'Father, I have sinned against heaven and against you. I am no longer worthy to be called your son.'

22 "But the father said to his servants, 'Quick! Bring the best
robe and put it on him. Put a ring on his finger and sandals on
his feet. 23 Bring the fattened calf and kill it. Let's have a feast
and celebrate. 24 For this son of mine was dead and is alive
again; he was lost and is found.' So they began to celebrate.
(Luke 15:17-22 NIV)

The prodigal son utilized his inner qualities and available resources—insight and self-awareness, spirit of repentance, humility, submission and willingness to serve—to attain a significant peace. This narrative illustrates a lesson on leveraging our inherent gifts for the benefit and harmony of everyone.

The ultimate peace (through salvation) between humanity and God, with Christ serving as our mediator, is also achieved through direct communication for anyone who calls upon Him in faith and repentance (Romans 13:10).

Like how the shortest distance between two points is typically a straight line, achieving authentic peace comes from mutual and unswerving truth that saves. And this liberating effect of truth

(John 8:32) is assured through direct, honest, and unfiltered dialogue between individuals.

Often, we find ourselves reacting similarly. Inundated and frustrated in difficulties, in relationship challenges or during other storms of life, we turn to Jesus only after having exhausted all other options that may have probably made difficult situation worse. Despite our efforts, if challenges continue to persist, we may feel overwhelmed and allow fear to undermine our confidence. This can lead us to doubt or question whether Jesus truly has control over our circumstances.

To lead an empowered and peaceful life, it is essential to live with intentionality, self-awareness and discernment. This involves taking control of our destinies casting our cares unto the Lord and making deliberate efforts to submit to God's leading to manage our affairs in ways that promote a peaceful existence. We should write our own narratives of peace with the word of God rather than allowing others to force us into living with resentment by reacting to their provocations, hurts, and insults with anger, rancour, and bitterness. Instead, we must respond in Godly ways that overcome negativity with positivity, for the sake of our peace and mental well-being.

Stephen R. Covey writes: ***"All things are created twice, but not all first creations are by conscious design."***

In our personal lives, if we do not develop our own self-awareness and become responsible for first creations, we empower other people and circumstances outside our Circle of Influence to shape much of our lives by default. Consequently, we tend to follow the predetermined roles and expectations imposed upon us by family, colleagues, external agendas, situational pressures, and possibly the influences of our early experiences, training, and conditioning.

From Moses to Joshua, Esther to King David, and Apostle Peter to Paul, their lives were marked by their intentional awareness of God's presence. Their peace came not from the absence of storms or temptation but through the understanding that true peace is only achievable with Christ, within or without storms.

LESSON FROM JOB IN HIS STORM

Described as blameless and upright (Job 1:1 NKJV), Job was a remarkable example of a man who, despite being visited with terror and darkness, exemplifies calm in crisis, weathering all storms of His unrelenting trials, trusting in God even against all odds. He was abandoned by his disapproving wife, who told him to curse God and die (Job 2:9-10). He then lost his wife and children, his health, his wealth, and all he worked for.

His 42-chapter story can easily read like this:

Chapter 1 He was a very wealthy God-fearing man known for his integrity and reverence, residing in the land of Uz.

In Chapter 2, God permitted temptation by the devil, which Job resisted, but he lost his wealth, health, and children.

In Chapter 42, Job's fortunes were not just restored; they were enhanced through the generous grace of God, as depicted below:

"Now the Lord blessed the latter days of Job more than his beginning; for he had fourteen thousand sheep, six thousand camels, one thousand yoke of oxen, and one thousand female donkeys. He also had seven sons and three daughters. In all the land were found no women so beautiful as the daughters of Job; and their father gave them an inheritance among their brothers.

After this Job lived one hundred and forty years, and saw his children and grandchildren for four generations. So Job died, old and full of days." (Job 42:12-13, 15-17 NKJV).

To know details of what happened and how if did, from chapters 3 through 41, read the book of Job for clarity and insight on:

- His trials and tribulations
- How he lost it all
- How he stayed calm amid such terror and darkness.
- How he got back all that he lost and ended up twice as much as he originally had, in riches.

Did job have unanswered questions. Was his patience tested? Did he experience sadness?

Overall, was Job at peace with God and did he have the peace of God? How did he do this?

Job faced many unresolved questions. His patience was severely tested, and he endured profound and challenging temptations and trials (Job 2:13, 3:1). These trials were extraordinarily intense; beyond what one might easily comprehend. Despite this, Job was not defined by his grief. Instead, his attitude and response to God demonstrated a man who:

- **Assessed** his situation with understanding and insight
- **Blessed** God with integrity and uprightness even in trials, and
- **Confessed** and proved his trust in a faithful God

Job never changed his mind about God, and God never changed His mind about Job. Job 13:15-16 best summarises Job's mindset and attitude to his storm:

"Though He slay me, yet will I trust Him. Even so, I will defend my own ways before Him. He also shall be my salvation, for a hypocrite could not come before Him." (Job 13:15-16 NKJV).

Although circumstances may be challenging, it is essential to maintain trust. If you find yourself in a situation that is difficult to comprehend, do not lose faith in either God or yourself. When your circumstances seem overwhelming, reflect on this significant promise from the Bible: **"You will keep him in perfect peace, whose mind is stayed on You, because he trusts in You. Trust in the Lord forever, for in... the Lord is everlasting strength"** (Isaiah 26:3-4 NKJV).

Trusting God does not mean He will answer all your questions, but that He will give you 'perfect peace' regardless of the circumstances.

Job serves as an illustration that God may permit storms and adversities in people's lives even when they have not committed any specific sin to "deserve" them. Hence, storms and suffering can be part of God's plan to purify and mature individuals. At peace with God during his trials, Job exemplifies patience and endurance through the testing of faith, allowing patience to achieve its perfect work, resulting in one being perfect and complete, lacking nothing.

The peace that endures during extreme trials and storms, while attainable by individuals, is not inherent to them. The following chapter provides insight into the type of peace that ensures calmness and a sense of security amidst challenges and adversities.

Chapter 4
THE PEACE OF GOD

THE PEACE OF GOD DEFINED

"and the PEACE OF GOD, which surpasses all understanding, will guard your hearts and minds through Christ Jesus." (Philippians 4:7 NKJV).

This type of peace transcends human understanding and capabilities, defying explanation by natural reasoning in our conflict-ridden world. To experience and sustain this level of peace, one must either become its originator or adopt the nature of the originator. It speaks of the kind of peace which does not always make sense to a natural man. It's usually difficult to explain:

This describes a state of tranquillity, calm, internal serenity, and emotional well-being that clearly exceeds the expectations of man, and what man can reason out or comprehend as humanly possible, marked by inner feeling of assuredness, contentment and control. This peace is usually associated with a sense of being secure even in challenging and humanly intolerable situations. It is divine, and it is therefore a gift from God. This kind of peace is called the peace of God.

Two scriptural scenarios that come to mind about this kind of peace:

1. IN LIFE THREATENED

Recall Jesus with His disciples in that Sea of Galilee boat to the other side of the lake, after He finished ministering to a throng of people, where boisterous wind threatened their safety and threw His disciples into fear and panic.

Remember where Jesus was and what He was doing in this boat in jeopardy:

- Jesus was deeply asleep on a pillow, in the stern.
- He was calm, undisturbed and in a tranquil state, whilst in potentially life-threatening situation.

Recall Jesus' response after they frantically awoke Him from sleep:

- He first stilled the raging sea with His "Peace Be Still" command to the element before turning to His disciples.
- Jesus was sane, considerate and compassionate enough to prioritise their safety first before His soul-searching question to them about their relationship with faith and fear.
- Though their question, "Teacher, do You not care that we are perishing," seemed accusatory, Jesus' response was gracious, suitable, restorative, and well-measured.

This peace is grounded in a confident assurance of the wisdom and power of a sovereign God, who operates in alignment with the righteous intentions of His will in all situations. This implies that we can, in faith, trust in the understanding that

He will indeed ensure that all things work together for our benefit (Romans 8:28) irrespective of what the reality on ground says.

2. IN DEATH SITUATION

AGAIN, in the book of John Chapter 11:1-44, a man of Bethany and a friend of the Lord, Lazarus, was very sick, unto death. While Lazarus' sisters, Mary and Mather were frightened and sent for the Messiah to come and heal him, fearing imminent death, Jesus' relaxed confidence meant he stayed two more days before he went to see Lazarus.

"So, when He heard that he (Lazarus) was sick, He stayed two more days in the place where He was. Then after this He said to the disciples, "Let us go to Judea again." (John 11:6-7 NKJV).

Lazarus had died and already four days (John 11: 17, 39) in the tomb by the time Jesus arrived to miraculously raise him from death.

"So when Jesus came, He found that he had already been in the tomb four days. Jesus said, "Take away the stone." Martha, the sister of him who was dead, said to Him, "Lord, by this time there is a stench, for he has been dead four days." Now when He had said these things, He cried with a loud voice, "Lazarus, come forth!" And he who had died came out bound hand and foot with grave clothes, and his face was wrapped with a cloth. Jesus said to them, "Loose him, and let him go."" (John 11:17, 39, 43-44 NKJV).

Looking at the two scenarios:

Despite the imminent threat and terrifying nature of the storm, and Lazarus's critical, end-of life condition, Christ displayed unwavering composure and confidence in the righteousness of God's plan. In both situations, Jesus remained calm and acted according to His timing, leading to a positive outcome.

This is the peace of God!

THE PEACE OF GOD EXPERIENCED

Having described the nature of peace that God possesses, the question arises: what is the significance of this peace if it only exists as a definition, is unattainable by humans, and cannot be transferred to individuals?

What value does this peace hold if individuals are unable to leverage it to live, interact, and collaborate harmoniously with others, thereby fostering peaceful marriages, homes, workplaces, and service experiences?

This peace is available to anyone with a prepared heart and mind, ready for the Holy Spirit's touch that guarantees peace to all believers.

KING DAVID EXPERIENCES A SEMBLANCE OF PEACE OF GOD.

David experienced challenging and life-threatening circumstances that tested his faith to the brink of compromise. Despite being relentlessly pursued by Saul, who sought to kill him out of fear and jealousy, David persistently refrained from taking revenge despite having multiple opportunities to do so and multiple opportunities to kill Saul (1 Samuel 24:1-22; 1 Samuel 26:2-25). This deliberate and spirit-inspired act of restraint, despite valid and justifiable reasons for retaliation against failed attempts on his life by Saul, exemplified his resilience, self-control, and Godly capacity to uphold peace in the face of danger and extreme provocation.

David also faced several personal challenges and family issues, which were further complicated by his son Absalom's act of rebellion and attempt to overthrow him, as well as incidents of incest and murder within his household.

Despite these, David could write:

"I will both lie down in peace, and sleep; For You alone, O Lord, make me dwell in safety." (Psalms 4:8 NKJV)

David's psalms offer a profound insight into an individual who understood where and how to seek peace and solace amidst life's challenges. His peace was not without adversity but within it, and it did not come from an absence of threats or obstacles, but rather from the reassuring presence of the Lord.

And for ELIJAH, it was this kind of peace that sustained and kept him afloat when his humanity and frailty showed up in his trying moments against the prophets of Baal.

Prophet Isaiah writes:

"You will guard him and keep him in perfect and constant peace whose mind [both its inclination and its character] is stayed on You, because he commits himself to You, leans on You, and hopes confidently in You." (Isaiah 26:3 AMPC)

Therefore, it is God who guards our hearts and minds, to direct our inner thoughts and emotions to Peacefulness according to Philippians 4:7.

The serenity of the soul necessitates the engagement of both our hearts and minds. As the author of peace, God works through them to provide us with tranquillity. However, attaining and experiencing this peace requires adherence to the directives outlined in the preceding verse Philippians 4:6:

"Be anxious for nothing, but in everything by prayer and supplication, with thanksgiving, let your requests be made known to God." (Philippians 4:6 NKJV)

This involves intentionality and choice - being deliberate about managing our worries and concerns and making informed decisions regarding what to accept and what to reject in our hearts and minds. It is about consciously deciding not to dwell on and internalize our anxieties, but rather purposefully submitting them to the appropriate authority - God, who can assist us and will, to effectively manage these concerns and provide help in times of need.

In a world where frictions are part of relationship-driven life and offences are inevitable; we have a choice to make on:

- How to avoid preventable and purposeless frictions.
- Manage frictions that are part of our journeys to growth, progress and character building.
- How to react to offences to retain our sanity and mental health.
- How to manage offences and transform them into opportunities for personal growth and improvement of others, including the offender(s).

AND THIS PEACE IS OURS TO TAKE

"Peace I leave with you, My peace I give to you; not as the world gives do I give to you. Let not your heart be troubled, neither let it be afraid." (John 14:27 NKJV).

The peace of God is bestowed upon us. When something is entrusted to someone, it implies a temporary custodial arrangement. However, when something is given, there is no expectation of its return. In this context, the Lord began with "My peace I leave with you" and concluded with "Peace I give to you," signifying that God has intentionally provided peace for us to receive and make our own permanently.

And of what use is this gift if we do not receive what is given?

Therefore, Paul further advises:

"And let the peace of Christ rule in your hearts, to which indeed you were called in one body. And be thankful" (Colossians 3:15).

THE CHURCH REQUIRES PEACE FOR INTERPERSONAL RELATIONSHIPS

In Philippians Chapter 4, the Apostle Paul addresses two believers, Euodia and Syntyche, who appear to be involved in a disagreement within the church. In this context, characterized by a lack of peace, he advises them to adopt the same mindset, specifically the mindset of Christ, to resolve their dispute and achieve harmony.

Paul gives this advice instead of taking sides or trying to solve their problem by human wisdom. He simply told them to be of the same mind in the Lord, an advice that is very clearly inspired by Divine wisdom of James 3:17:

"But the wisdom from above is always pure, filled with peace, considerate and teachable. It is filled with love and never displays prejudice or hypocrisy in any form and it always bears the beautiful harvest of righteousness! Good seeds of wisdom's

fruit will be planted with peaceful acts by those who cherish making peace." (James 3:17-18 TPT)

To be of the same mind in the Lord: Whatever the dispute was about, Euodia and Syntyche were reminded that their shared belief in Jesus Christ was significant. They were encouraged to view everything else as less important than that common ground. This is a lesson for us in having the mind of Christ, which enables us to esteem one another in a loving way that guarantees accord and peace (Philippians 2:2-4).

Subsequently, addressing the Philippian Church, which seems to require assistance on the topic of peace, Paul offers additional advice and guidance on how to attain this peace:

"Do not be anxious or worried about anything, but in everything [every circumstance and situation] by prayer and petition with thanksgiving, continue to make your [specific] requests known to God. And the peace of God [that peace which reassures the heart, that peace] which transcends all understanding, [that peace which] stands guard over your hearts and your minds in Christ Jesus [is yours]." (Philippians 4:6-7 AMP)

And this is how Amplified Classic captures it:

"Do not fret or have any anxiety about anything, but in every circumstance and in everything, by prayer and petition (definite requests), with thanksgiving, continue to make your wants known to God. And God's peace [shall be yours, that tranquil state of a soul assured of its salvation through Christ, and so fearing nothing from God and being content with its earthly lot of whatever sort that is, that peace] which transcends all

understanding shall garrison and mount guard over your hearts and minds in Christ Jesus." (Philippians 4:6-7 AMPC)

Jesus is called the Lord of peace (2 Thessalonians 3:16), the Prince of peace (Isaiah 9:6), the author of peace (John 16:33) and the giver of peace (John 14:27).

And Jesus is our peace and the scripture says so:

"For He Himself is our peace, who has made both one, and has broken down the middle wall of separation," (Ephesians 2:14 NKJV).

SUBMITTING TO GOD AND KNOWING HIM IS ROUTE TO THIS PEACE

If God is peace, then to know God is to know peace and to bask in His peace. The closer we draw to Him, therefore, the more of His peace we can enjoy (James 4:8). The need to draw closer to our God is informed by our sinful nature.

"As the Scriptures say, "No one is righteous— not even one. For everyone has sinned, we all fall short of God's glorious standard." (Romans 3:10, 23 NLT)

The righteousness we have is not one we accomplished by ourselves: we do not earn it. It is God that makes righteous and it's his righteousness that He accounts to us.

"For He made Him who knew no sin to be sin for us, that we might become the righteousness of God in Him." (2 Corinthians 5:21 NKJV)

With righteousness accounted to us, the life we live should be as though Adam did not sin - because we all have accounted righteousness.

For example, one of the last acts committed by Saul in the biblical narrative is described as follows:

"But Stephen, full of the Holy Spirit, gazed steadily into heaven and saw the glory of God, and he saw Jesus standing in the place of honour at God's right hand. And he told them, "Look, I see the heavens opened and the Son of Man standing in the place of honour at God's right hand!" and dragged him out of the city and began to stone him. His accusers took off their coats and laid them at the feet of a young man named Saul. As they stoned him, Stephen prayed, "Lord Jesus, receive my spirit." He fell to his knees, shouting, "Lord, don't charge them with this sin!" And with that, he died." (Acts 7:55-56, 58-60 NLT)

Paul killed and maimed believers, until God stopped him on his way to repeat this in Damascus. His involvement in killing included Stephen's death.

And below is the testimony of the same Paul after he repented and had righteousness of God accounted to him:

"Therefore, I testify to you this day that I am innocent of the blood of all men." (Acts 20:26 NKJV)

He is now washed and cleaned; he recognised this in his second letter to the Corinthians chapter 5, where he is bold to declare thus:

"Therefore, if anyone is in Christ, he is a new creation; old things have passed away; behold, all things have become new." (2 Corinthians 5:17 NKJV)

And as long as your heart is stayed on God as a transformed person who has submitted his or her life to our saviour, Christ's peace will be yours.

"You will keep him in perfect peace, Whose mind is stayed on You, Because he trusts in You." (Isaiah 26:3 NKJV)

I pray God to give you grace for a perfect heart that is trustfully stayed on Him in all situations so that your peace can be multidimensional in all situations – amen.

The Attributes of PEACE OF GOD

- It is beyond human understanding and does not make sense to a carnal man who works based on the prompting of the flesh
- This peace is rooted in our inner man authored by the spirit (Galatians 5:22-23) and guards our hearts and mind with all diligence, to keeps them from being overcome by mundane care, disabling worries and anxiety, even in difficult times and circumstances.
- It is divine and comes from God, meaning you need PEACE WITH GOD to have the peace of God.

It takes revelation and divine insight with *supernaturalness* and omniscience to react the way Jesus did during the potentially life-threatening storm and in Lazarus' situation. As a God that knows the end from the beginning (Isaiah 46:10), from whom nothing is hidden (Hebrews 4:13), and who gives us insight through the word (John 14:26; John 16:13) and revelation of secret things (Deuteronomy 29:29), we gain the confidence and faith to react like Him when we submit to Him and He blesses us with His nature and character.

To operate in or with this kind of peace, one must therefore walk in confident assurance that one is a friend of God and abiding in Him, guaranteeing reciprocal abiding and relationship that empowers one to reap the dividends of the relationship, one of which is the peace of God.

To have the PEACE OF GOD therefore, you need to be at PEACE WITH GOD, which in detail, is what the next chapter is all about.

Chapter 5
PEACE WITH GOD

The concept of Peace with God takes into consideration, the truth of existence of enmity between a holy God and a sinful, untransformed and unsaved man.

Isaiah writes:

"Behold, the Lord's hand is not shortened, That it cannot save; Nor His ear heavy, That it cannot hear. But your iniquities have separated you from your God; And your sins have hidden His face from you, So that He will not hear." (Isaiah 59:1-2 NKJV)

THE OFFENCE and THE RESULT

Sin is offensive to a holy God and sin is a separator that puts distance between this holy God who cannot behold iniquity (Habakkuk 1:3) and a sinful man, whose connection with Adam, means he is by origin and nature, contaminated with sin.

To understand the need for peace with God, therefore, we must recognize that humans in our natural, sinful state are enemies of God.

It all began with the sin of Adam and Eve (Read Genesis 3:1-24).

THE ENMITY & GENESIS 3:15 IN CONTEXT:

"And I will put enmity Between you and the woman, And between your seed and her Seed; He shall bruise your head, And you shall bruise His heel." (Genesis 3:15 NKJV)

Consider the insight of the above passage. God, in Genesis 2:16-17, warned:

"Of every tree of the garden you may freely eat; but of the tree of the knowledge of good and evil you shall not eat, for in the day that you eat of it you shall surely die."" (Genesis 2:16-17 NKJV).

The initial effect of sin is non-physical death, characterized by spiritual separation from God. This separation leads humans and individuals to distance themselves from a holy God, resulting from the disruption of spiritual relationships caused by the nature of sin.

And words about their physical death which will come later, is spoken of just a few verses down the passage, in Genesis 3:19.

"In the sweat of your face you shall eat bread Till you return to the ground, For out of it you were taken; For dust you are, and to dust you shall return." (Genesis 3:19 NKJV)

Here, God presented the man with Eve, his helpmeet, who the serpent seduced to take from the tree and eat. She gave the fruit to the man, and both hid when they heard God approaching (Genesis 3:8). **Why were they hiding?**

1) Due to their fall and sin acting as a separator, they were driven away from Him.
2) They feared death, the clearly pre-warned consequence of their fall.

And to the serpent in Genesis 3:15, God said:

"And I will put enmity Between you and the woman, And between your seed and her Seed; He shall bruise your head, And you shall bruise His heel."

This judgement is considered the "first gospel" that introduces the theme of a future saviour who will redeem the world from the curse of sin (Galatians 3:13). The saviour, who is Jesus Christ, is described as the "Seed" of the woman who will redeem the world from the curse of sin.

All humans therefore need a savour and PEACE WITH GOD because:

"When Adam sinned, the entire world was affected. Sin entered human experience, and death was the result. And so death followed this sin, casting its shadow over all humanity, because all have sinned." (Romans 5:12 TPT)

Therefore, because we inherited a sin nature from our first parents, Adam and Eve (Genesis 3, Romans 5:12), we are born with a disposition to please ourselves and be our own gods. That rebellious nature sets us at odds with our perfect Creator. Because His just nature cannot overlook our sin; justice demands punishment (Romans 3:23, 6:23), for atonement and redemption from the consequence of sin. We are unable to create peace with God because our best efforts on our best day are nothing, but filthy rags compared to His holiness (Isaiah 64:6).

"We are all infected and impure with sin. When we display our righteous deeds, they are nothing but filthy rags. Like autumn leaves, we wither and fall, and our sins sweep us away like the wind." (Isaiah 64:6 NLT)

In our flawed state, we are incapable of achieving salvation or reconciliation, nor can we attain peace with God through our efforts alone. To be reconciled with God and achieve peace, we require a saviour, and that saviour is Christ, who saves us by Grace and counts us righteous, not because of our works, but because of their faith in Him and in His finished work (death) on the cross of Calvary.

"We are saved by special grace of God through acts of faith, not by our works and not by law-keeping." (Ephesians 2:8)

"But people are counted as righteous, not because of their work, but because of their faith in God who forgives sinners." (Romans 4:5 NLT)

Through our faith in Christ's death, our old man (nature) living in sin is counted as dead to sin, and through faith in Christ's resurrection one is resurrected into new man, with a transformed life that is now counted as righteous (Galatians 6:4).

Peace with God and humanity is achieved through Christ's blood and death on the cross (Colossians 1:20). As High Priest, Jesus sustains this friendship for believers who approach God through him, as he eternally intercedes for them (Hebrews 7:25). Viewed from another perspective, according to Colossians 1:20, reconciliation between God and humanity is said to have been accomplished through Jesus Christ's blood and sacrificial death on the cross. Additionally, Hebrews 7:25 states that as the High Priest, Jesus maintains this relationship for those who continue to approach God through Him, as He always lives to make intercession for them.

This state of friendship with God is therefore a prerequisite for the earlier described kind of peace which comes with tranquil mind - the PEACE OF GOD.

It is only when our relationship with God is made right through confession of our sins, our repentance from them with forgiveness of our iniquities through the grace of our saviour, Christ, that we can have peace with God

"Therefore, since we have been made right in God's sight by faith, we have PEACE WITH GOD because of what Jesus Christ our Lord has done for us." (Romans 5:1).

Once we have peace with God, the Holy Spirit lives in us, enabling us to show the fruits of a life submitted to God as described in Galatians 5:22-23:

"But the Holy Spirit produces this kind of fruit in our lives: love, joy, peace, patience, kindness, goodness, faithfulness, gentleness, and self-control. There is no law against these things!" (Galatians 5:22-23 NLT).

This enduring peace withstands the test of time as we reside in a world where the creator is recognized as the Lord of peace.

"Now may the Lord of peace Himself give you peace always in every way. The Lord be with you all." (2 Thessalonians 3:16 NKJV).

To be at peace with God, one must therefore:

- Draw near to Him (James 4:8).
- Accept Him as Lord and personal saviour (Romans 10:10-13; 1 John 4:10).
- Fellowship with Him and build intimacy with Him through fellowship.
- Seek the Helper He gives - the Holy Spirit the inspires unto good works and peace.
- Abide in in His words and the leading of the holy spirit that guides us to live in peace with others.

Psalm 24:3-4 (NLT) teaches us how to draw near to God:

"Who may climb the mountain of the Lord? Who may stand in his holy place? Only those whose hands and hearts are pure, who do not worship idols and never tell lies. They will receive the Lord's blessing and have a right relationship with God their savior. Such people may seek you and worship in your presence, O God of Jacob. Interlude".

As we work to pursue peace with all men as much as depends on us and lead lives that are congruent with His Character as God of Peace, chapter 6 will focus on the **ABC of peace** that adopts a contextual approach to evaluating peace disruptors that challenge us and provides guidance on inspired responses, to ensure these challenges are overcome positively, so that overall, all parties involved benefit from the outcome.

Chapter 6
THE ABC OF ENDURING PEACE

"These things I have spoken to you, that in Me you may have peace. In the world you will have tribulation; but be of good cheer, I have overcome the world." (John 16:33 NKJV).

It is evident that we will encounter situations that can challenge our peace of mind as long as we live in this world. Children may push boundaries; spouses may cause misunderstandings or annoyance, and traffic situations can test one's patience during the commute.

In the workplace, misunderstandings and conflicts are likely to occur, and expectations may sometimes be unrealistic. Additionally, colleagues or supervisors may fall short of expectations, and instances of bullying, whether intentional or not, may arise. Within the community, individuals may act unkindly, offenses may occur, leaders may disappoint, and friends may inadvertently or intentionally betray trust.

In places of worship, the messages may not always align with your preferences, and some teachings may provoke strong reactions (Acts 7:54). You may encounter individuals and behaviours that challenge your expectations, and you might witness actions that test your beliefs. In some cases, leaders may present controversial doctrines or engage in behaviours that conflict with established principles.

Your response to these experiences can significantly impact your sense of peace. Do you address them with understanding and empathy, or do you react with anger, frustration, judgement or the wisdom of discernment? The response you choose will determine the outcome you get. In your home, workplace, or places of worship, there is usually a standard rule on how to respond, and this, done with wisdom in most appropriate and timely manner means your peace is guaranteed.

For a systematic method of addressing potential disturbances to peace, I propose the ABC of Peace. This approach outlines a framework for responding to triggers in a manner that fosters and maintains peace through:

1) **ASSESSING** the situation considering the gospel.
2) **BLESSING** the offender or situation in preference to hating it.
3) **CONFESSING** with your attitudes, actions and words that edify, as the light of the world.

A genuine life of peace is not lived in isolation. It is achieved through our interactions with individuals of all classes, creed, genders and ages, within a community comprising diverse personalities, temperaments, emotions, and agendas. This encompasses experiences that challenge us as well as our engagements in homes, workplaces, public spaces, and other environments where humans interact.

Therefore, for a truly guaranteed life of peace, one must be intentional about a life that's truly empowered for victorious living that impacts self and others in the following environments and relationships:

- Homes and families.
- Workplaces.
- Our community.
- Places of service or worship.

The ABC of peace is a template that helps us to manage circumstances that disturb our peace. It essentially guides our reaction to adversities, helping us to deal with storm-producing situations that are capable of unsettling or undermining our sense of safety. It represents a system, which although is a template or guide, physically, should meticulously be applied with a mind that's guided, not by human thinking, but spiritual introspection, grace and love.

A stand for ASSESS - the situation or person

B stands for BLESS - the situation or person

C stands for CONFESS - with your actions and attitude

ASSESSING the situation or person

"Examine yourselves to see if your faith is genuine. Test yourselves. Surely you know that Jesus Christ is among you; if not, you have failed the test of genuine faith." (2 Corinthians 13:5 NLT).

When in the storm, the stern of your life, or in your personal Sea of Galilea, one very important thing to do in pursuit of peace is to first assess the situation. This is an opportunity to pause and contemplate, to ask critical questions about how you got to this point. Reflect on the root causes of the challenge or the circumstances leading to it, including your role, actions, or inactions prior to the experience. Prepare for your responses based on the insights gained from your assessment.

Impulsive responses to challenging situations often result in errors and poor judgments, potentially worsening the circumstances. Evaluating the situation allows for thoughtful reactions, which can lead to better outcomes through careful discernment.

Questions that come under here include:

- How did I get here?
- What's my role if any in this?
- How would God see this situation and what would be His reaction?
- What lesson is intended here?

CASE SCENARIO - The Prodigal Son

Back to the story of the prodigal son in Luke 15. After coming to his senses, he assessed his situation, realizing he lost peace due to wasting his inheritance through fiscal recklessness.

Luke writes:

"When he finally came to his senses, he said to himself, 'At home even the hired servants have food enough to spare, and here I am dying of hunger! I will go home to my father and say, "Father, I have sinned against both heaven and you, and I am no longer worthy of being called your son. Please take me on as a hired servant."' "So he returned home to his father. And while he was still a long way off, his father saw him coming. Filled with love and compassion, he ran to his son, embraced him, and kissed him. His son said to him, 'Father, I have sinned against

both heaven and you, and I am no longer worthy of being called your son.' "But his father said to the servants, 'Quick! Bring the finest robe in the house and put it on him. Get a ring for his finger and sandals for his feet. And kill the calf we have been fattening. We must celebrate with a feast, for this son of mine was dead and has now returned to life. He was lost, but now he is found.' So the party began." (Luke 15:17-24 NLT)

The prodigal son required a thorough self-assessment and situational evaluation to recognize his mistakes and address the misconceptions that led him away from discipline and honour, and towards indulgence, disgrace, and discontentment. Once he acknowledged his unworthiness and took responsibility for his lack of peace, he implemented actions that restored him to a successful path and into the welcoming embrace of his loving and forgiving father.

Confessing our failings and sins to God, who is referred to as our PEACE (Ephesians 2:14), requires self-assessment.

If we claim to be without sin, "**we deceive ourselves and the truth is not in us**" (1 John 1:8). It is harmful to lie to ourselves. The prodigal son, however, honestly assessed his life and situation, leading to a positive outcome for him and his family.

Beware of Prejudices

While reflective and corrective self-assessment or situation evaluation is crucial in our pursuit of peace during challenging times, especially when we are at fault, it is important to ensure that this does not become an unhealthy practice of self-condemnation or an opportunity to unjustly judge others.

The scriptural story in John chapter 9, of a man born blind from birth speaks of an attempt by Christ's disciples to ASSESS a situation that caused them some concerns and most likely disturbed the peace of the blind man and his family. The man's relatives most certainly would like an answer for closure and for peace, even though the question and curiosity emanated from the disciples.

John writes:

"Rabbi," his disciples asked him, "why was this man born blind? Was it because of his own sins or his parents' sins?" "It was not because of his sins or his parents' sins," Jesus answered. "This happened so the power of God could be seen in him. We must quickly carry out the tasks assigned us by the one who sent us. The night is coming, and then no one can work. But while I am here in the world, I am the light of the world." Then he spit on the ground, made mud with the saliva, and spread the mud over the blind man's eyes. He told him, "Go wash yourself in the pool of Siloam" (Siloam means "sent"). So the man went and washed and came back seeing!" (John 9:2-7 NLT)

The goal of assessment and self-examination is to discover truth, for lasting peace. Inspired truth helps us respond in ways that ensure enduring peace and freedom from the burdens of our challenges.

It is important to understand that the man's blindness was not caused by any sin of his own or that of his parents. This realization should bring them peace and alleviate any feelings of guilt. Moreover, Jesus explained that even this affliction was part of His divine plan so that God's work could be manifested in him, thereby glorifying God. While it may be appropriate to engage in self-reflection during periods of adversity, it is important to do so with discernment, avoiding judgments about the reasons for others' suffering. Rather, we should focus on responding with compassion and grace. It is evident that Christ did not prioritize religious explanations for suffering; instead, He emphasized the importance of our response, which is why He chose to heal rather than to judge.

BLESSING the situation, the person or yourself

"Do not let evil defeat you; instead, conquer evil with good." (Romans 12:21 GNBUK).

Situations that disrupt our peace can be either neutral or negative, but they often result in outcomes that are not beneficial. Although these experiences may sometimes lead to positive, unintended results, their typical outcome is usually the emergence of negative emotions. These unsettling situations disrupt our internal equilibrium and tranquillity by causing distressing and unhealthy feelings of stress, worry, anxiety, or panic. They negatively impact our thoughts and emotions, thereby distorting our sense of peace.

By learning how unsettling experiences undermine our sense of calm, we can learn or develop coping strategies that can lead us to (or restore our) peace.

John Writes:

"The thief's purpose is to steal and kill and destroy. My purpose is to give them a rich and satisfying life." (John 10:10 NLT)

Whereas God's purpose is for righteous self-assessment outcome that blesses, the devil's favourite trick is to destroy our testimony and peace by whispering false assurance to a culpable and unrepentant heart. Without the guidance of holy Spirit, instead of an honest self-assessment outcome that blesses with truth that saves, we end with the devil's lie that sounds pleasant, plausible and too palatable to challenge on our own.

For the prodigal son, his action following his assessment of the situation was inspired by truth that:

- Blessed him with Godly sorrow and a genuine heart of contrition (2 Corinthians 7:9-10) that led to his repentance.
- Blessed his family with restoration of the lost son that was found, into the loving embrace of his family (Luke 15:24).
- Blessed heaven that gained a soul with added joy over a sinner with a changed heart (Luke 15:7 & 10)

In a situation where there is no one to blame for an unsettling situation that threatens to steal your peace, derive your sense of calm and hope by the assurance of Romans 8:30, which says:

"And we know that God causes everything to work together for the good of those who love God and are called according to his purpose for them." (Romans 8:28 NLT)

Consider it joy by reflecting on the message from James 1:2-4, which states:

"Dear brothers and sisters, when troubles of any kind come your way, consider it an opportunity for great joy. For you know that when your faith is tested, your endurance has a chance to grow. So let it grow, for when your endurance is fully developed, you will be perfect and complete, needing nothing." (James 1:2-4 NLT)

Similarly, rather than engaging in continuous self-blame or guilt that may lead to a depressed mood, it is beneficial to acknowledge your role in the situation, forgive yourself, and move forward. This approach aligns with the guidance provided in 1 John 1:9 and Philippians 3:13-14.

"If we say that we have no sin, we deceive ourselves, and the truth is not in us. If we confess our sins, He is faithful and just to forgive us our sins and to cleanse us from all unrighteousness." (I John 1:8-9 NKJV)

and

"Brothers and sisters, I do not consider that I have made it my own yet; but one thing I do: forgetting what lies behind and reaching forward to what lies ahead, I press on toward the goal to win the [heavenly] prize of the upward call of God in Christ Jesus." (Philippians 3:13-14 AMP)

If you're struggling with unforgiving behaviour towards others or those who have offended you, be ready to bless and regain your peace through forgiveness.

"Be kind and helpful to one another, tender-hearted [compassionate, understanding], forgiving one another [readily and freely], just as God in Christ also forgave you." (Ephesians 4:32 AMP)

And Joseph BLESSED his brothers with FORGIVENESS

These were his brothers that planned to kill him so that he would not live to rule over them as his dream suggested, but they ended up selling him to the Midianites (Genesis 37:12-36).

The scriptural account:

"When Joseph's brothers saw that their father was dead, they said, "Perhaps Joseph will hate us, and may actually repay us for all the evil which we did to him." So they sent messengers to Joseph, saying, "Before your father died he commanded, saying, 'Thus you shall say to Joseph: "I beg you, please forgive the trespass of your brothers and their sin; for they did evil to

you."' Now, please, forgive the trespass of the servants of the God of your father." And Joseph wept when they spoke to him. Then his brothers also went and fell down before his face, and they said, "Behold, we are your servants." Joseph said to them, "Do not be afraid, for am I in the place of God? But as for you, you meant evil against me; but God meant it for good, in order to bring it about as it is this day, to save many people alive. Now therefore, do not be afraid; I will provide for you and your little ones." And he comforted them and spoke kindly to them." (Genesis 50:15-21 NKJV)

<u>CONFESS with your attitudes, actions and words</u>

Joseph's brothers acknowledged the wrongdoing they committed against him and were concerned about the consequences they might face. They feared the justice and appropriate penalties that Joseph, holding a position of authority in Egypt, was capable of administering. Instead of seeking retribution, Joseph chose mercy and forgiveness, restoring his family to a place of reconciliation and peace. He demonstrated that we can make peace with our offenders as much as depends on us, by overcoming evil with good (Romans 12:18, Romans 12:21).

For with the heart, one believes unto righteousness, and with the mouth confession is made unto salvation. (Romans 10:10)

Under confess are two aspects which are partly contained in the previous part(s):

1) Confess through admission
2) Confess by declaration

We confess through our righteous words, actions, attitudes, and non-verbal cues such as body language, facial expressions, and tone of voice.

Confess by Admission

To confess is to admit that one has committed a crime or done something wrong. In scenario that threatens one's peace, nothing facilitates peace faster than the admission of wrong, mistake or crime.

Take the prodigal son for instance whose joy and peace were stolen by lustful and prodigal living:

- He ASSESSED the situation and came to the knowledge of truth of his failings.
- He BLESSED by his acts of repentance that changed his life, restored his relationship with both God and man, including his return to his family.
- He CONFESSED by admitting it before God and man.

Declarative Confession

We confess our faith by declaring its values and its impactful tenets, trusting in God. When our peace is threatened or when in the middle of storm or our Sea of Galilee, we can derive PEACE and find grace to help us remain calm by confessing our faith positively.

This explains Jeremiah's message to reassure anxious and worried Jews exiled in Babylon for over 70 years of God's promise:

"For I know the thoughts that I think toward you, says the Lord, thoughts of peace and not of evil, to give you a future and a hope." (Jeremiah 29:11 NKJV)

The Jews exiled in Babylon experienced what they perceived as God's judgment upon Israel. Having forgotten God's words, promises, and faithfulness, they became despondent about their situation and God's plan for them during exile. They might have thought that God was against them. Consequently, they lost their peace. Through Jeremiah, God reminded them that His thoughts toward them remained unchanged, emphasizing peace, a hopeful future, and good intentions for them.

During challenging periods in our lives, whether in marriage, work, family trials, or health issues, we can take comfort in and CONFESS the unwavering assurance of an unchanging God who promises a future filled with peace, hope, and prosperity.

Esther an example

When their PEACE was stolen by the storm of existential threat, all it took was for Esther (Jewish wife to the king) to make a declarative CONFESSION of her trust in God who is mighty to save; who has the hearts of kings (including Ahasuerus) in his hands, and then present herself uninvited (which was against the law and punishable by death) before the king (read the book of ESTHER for details).

The scriptural account:

"And in every province where the king's command and decree arrived, there was great mourning among the Jews, with fasting, weeping, and wailing; and many lay in sackcloth and ashes...And Mordecai told them to answer Esther: "Do not think in your heart that you will escape in the king's palace any more than all the other Jews. For if you remain completely silent at this time, relief and deliverance will arise for the Jews from another place, but you and your father's house will perish. Yet who knows whether you have come to the kingdom for such a time as this?" Then Esther told them to reply to Mordecai: "Go, gather all the Jews who are present in Shushan, and fast for me; neither eat nor drink for three days, night or day. My maids and

I will fast likewise. And so I will go to the king, which is against the law; and if I perish, I perish!"" (Esther 4:3, 13-16 NKJV)

Grace smiled on her as she found favour before the king:

And the king said to her, "What do you wish, Queen Esther? What is your request? It shall be given to you—up to half the kingdom!"" (Esther 5:3 NKJV)

Esther's declarative confession with the people's prayer worked. The king looked favourably on Esther whose life was spared; the evil plot was reversed with Mordecai honoured for the good he did. The plotter and mastermind of the evil, Haman, was hanged on the gallows and the Jewish people were saved from extinction.

There is power in faith and faith can move mountains, for it's the giver of faith (God) who works in us to will and to do (Philippians 2:13) all things through Christ who strengthens us (Philippians 4:13).

Paul would go ahead to tell Philippians that submitting to God's divine plan and purposes, CONFESSING Him even at any cost is the way to live fulfilling life (of peace here and in the life after), and just like Esther, Paul submitted:

"For to me, to live is Christ and to die is gain." (Philippians 1:21)

Paul's message to Philippians is still relevant today. We need peace to live Christian life and to impact the world, and for us to impact the world with peace, we must have peace that starts within. Chapter 7 speaks of peace within - that inner peace which then flows to the outside to impact those who our lives, as the light of the world, touch.

Chapter 7

THE PEACE WITHIN - INNER PEACE WITH YOURSELF

Inner peace is a fundamental prerequisite for achieving peace in multiple external dimensions.

Inner peace refers to a state of mental calmness and tranquillity that is internal. It involves focusing on one's natural energy, maintaining composure, and finding rest within oneself (in Christ). This state is accessible to everyone at any time, depending on where they direct their focus and it begins the moment you choose not to allow another person, external circumstances, situations or events to control your emotions.

It is important to apply the principle of ABC of peace for maintaining peaceful co-existence with others, especially in challenging relationship situations, to ensure a win-win outcome for all involved.

The wisdom of the scripture is clear on this:

"Make every effort to keep yourselves united in the Spirit, binding yourselves together with peace." (Ephesians 4:3 NLT).

"And let the peace of Christ rule in your hearts, to which indeed you were called in one body. And be thankful." (Colossians 3:15 ESV).

Your role notwithstanding, this is an inspired ability because human emotion is subject to what he hears, sees, experiences and the things that happen around him. Unless guided by the Holy Spirit Which God guarantees (2 Corinthians 5:5), to provide us with the desire and ability (Philippians 2:13) for inner peace, we are unable to have it, and 2 Corinthians 3:5 agrees, which says:

"**Not that we are sufficiently qualified in ourselves to claim anything as coming from us, but our sufficiency and qualifications come from God."**

This peace should have little or nothing to do with external surrounding and it is further defined by who you are and your perception of yourself. It involves a profound journey of self-acceptance, self-compassion, and establishing healthy personal boundaries. It means refusing to let external influences define your sense of self-worth, and instead, embracing your unique identity and inherent value from creation.

The John 14:27, **"Peace I leave with you; my peace I give to you,"** declaration also represents Christ's promise of peace for us to uphold and internalize, for our well-being in our journey of faith.

This peace is a fruit of the Holy Spirit (Galatians 5:22) as already established. When the "God of all peace" comes to live inside a believing heart (1 Corinthians 6:19), He begins to produce His own values and characteristics in that life, one of which includes inner peace that has little to do with external surroundings. We saw this in Jesus' Sea of Galilee experience where His peace was clearly undisturbed by the external storm and wave. Unaffected by the loud wind and waves, he was awakened by the quieter sound from his calling disciples and He responded as a good, loving shepherd (John 10:7-28) would, who hears his flock even before they cry.

The Psalmist concurs:

"It shall come to pass that before they call, I will answer, and while they are still speaking, I will hear." (Psalm 65:24 NJKV).

Inner peace comes from knowing that circumstances are temporary and that God is sovereign over all (Isaiah 46:9-11). Peace within comes from exercising faith in the character of God and His Word. We can have peace during challenges when we remember that **"all things work together for good to those who love God and who are called according to His purpose"** (Romans 8:28).

We can choose peace rather than give way to fear and worry. Inner peace resulting from a relationship with God allows us to keep things in proper perspective. We can therefore accept difficult situations on earth to His glory by remembering that our most important citizenship is not earthly, but in heaven (Philippians 3:20).

Authentic inner peace originates from a deep sense of self-assurance, fostering confidence in one's instincts and decision-making that is consistent with one's spiritual beliefs. It also necessitates recognizing the inevitability of life's continuous changes and cultivating the ability to adapt gracefully. Embracing the inner peace Christ has given us involves developing a non-judgmental attitude, showing compassion to oneself and others, and recognizing that each person has his or her own journey.

Furthermore, it entails acknowledging that life seldom progresses exactly as anticipated and attaining tranquillity through that acceptance. Fostering an attitude of gratitude for even the most minor blessing in life constitutes an essential component of this transformative journey toward inner peace. Difficulties or adversities can often challenge your inner peace, similar to the situation Christ faced while on the boat in the Sea of Galilee, but for every trials or challenges, there are opportunities for wins.

Three tips for staying calm during adversities:

1) FACE REALITY – All things work together for good, and problems happen for a reason (Romans 8:28)
    - Reality is the foundation of growth - telling yourself the truth and be honest with how to deal with them
    - Do not pretend as if they are not there.
    - The first responsibility is to define reality.
    - When you realise you are riding a dead horse, the best strategy is to dismount.
2) BELIEVE IN YOURSELF – You have the power within you to overcome (Philippians 2:13)
    - This does not mean trusting in your ability & not trusting in God.
    - Do not be overcome by self-doubt, but trust in your God-given ability to perform.
    - It's impossible to perform on the outside if on the inside you are overwhelmed by self-doubt.
    - Success can be achieved even if others do not believe in you, but it is unattainable if you lack self-belief.
3) MAKE INSPIRED DECISIONS - before (B) and during (D) ADVERSITY

- Don't make important decisions when in the valley - when your vision is clouded by the emotions of the moment (B).
- You need to plan against adversity before you have adversity (B).
- The best way to manage the problems of tomorrow is to prepare for the solution today (B).
- Trust in the Lord for Guidance and in all your ways acknowledge him in the wisdom of Proverbs 3:5-6 (B & D)
- Prayerfully take a step of faith whatever it may be, to address the adversity (D), because faith without work is dead (James 2:26).

The Good news is that the adversity will end and the Egyptians you see today will be there no more, and God will keep you safe and in peace.

"In peace I will lie down and sleep, for you alone, O Lord, will keep me safe." (Psalms 4:8 NLT).

The concept of adversity highlights the importance of different forms of peace, where individuals have specific roles to play in maintaining or restoring peace.

ENFORCED PEACE

In his address during our Peace Month in April 2025, Pastor Akin Kunlipe, the Lead Pastor and spiritual leader at Redeemed Christian Church of God, Canterbury, described this as taking proactive measures against challenges or adversities that threaten to undermine our peace, including, spiritual battle against:

- Sicknesses
- Failures in marriages

- Joblessness
- Subfertility
- Failure at the edge of success
- Unfounded fear of the unknown
- Ungodly family trends and patterns
- Challenges with raising children

He suggested that preparation before adversity strikes is crucial, as it is not a matter of if, but when, the adversary will attack. The mission of this adversary, whose actions are described in John 10:10, is to kill, steal, and destroy. Therefore, it is imperative to be ready for these challenges.

Sun Tzu captures this perfectly:

"The art of war teaches us to rely not on the likelihood of the enemy's not coming, but on our own readiness to receive him; not on the chance of his not attacking, but rather on the fact that we have made our position unassailable."

Thankfully we have divine promise from a God who is eternal and unchanging to fight our battle and give us peace (Exodus 14:14).

The same God also says:

"I will give you peace in the land, and you will be able to sleep with no cause for fear. I will rid the land of wild animals and keep your enemies out of your land. In fact, you will chase down your enemies and slaughter them with your swords. Five of you will chase a hundred, and a hundred of you will chase ten thousand! All your enemies will fall beneath your sword. "I will look favourably upon you, making you fertile and multiplying your people. And I will fulfil my covenant with you." (Leviticus 26:6-9 NLT)

The fact that what happens in the physical world is controlled in the spiritual realm as exemplified by Israel's victory in the battlefield against the Amalekites because of the spiritual activity (prayer) of Moses, Aaron and Hur on the mountain (Exodus 17:8-13), we need to prepare and fight the enemy with spiritual weapon of our warfare (2 Corinthians 10:3-5) and take captive to the obedience of Christ, any idea or thought that threatens to go contrary to God's purpose or this call for enforced peace.

Through her faith and relentless persistence against all odds and discouragements, the woman with the issue of blood took the battle to the enemy's camp for enforced peace after suffering a great deal at the hands of physicians (Mark 5:25-34). Divine compassion smiled on her, with healing and peace from the Lord as captured in Mark 5:34:

"And He said to her, "Daughter, your faith has made you well. Go in peace and be healed of your affliction."

The Apostle, Paul, for this reason, advises believers to "put on the full armour of God, so that you can make your stand against the devil's schemes" (Ephesians 6:11). This armour comprises truth, faith, **the gospel of peace**, righteousness, salvation and the word of God, all of which are crucial for remaining steadfast against spiritual adversaries.

Spiritual war and conflict are a part of life, but the Bible offers comfort and guidance. It teaches that God is our source of strength and victory, equipping us for battles and promising His presence and protection. In difficult times, we can trust in His plan for justice and reconciliation.

Paul's message to the Ephesians, still relevant today, highlights the need for spiritual readiness to face inevitable battles. This preparation enables Christians to resist temptation, overcome trials, and stay steadfast in their faith.

PROVOKED PEACE

This is the kind of peace that follows obedience to the word of God.

Paul writes on this peace:

"Be anxious for nothing, but in everything by prayer and supplication, with thanksgiving, let your requests be made known to God; and the peace of God, which surpasses all understanding, will guard your hearts and minds through Christ Jesus." (Philippians 4:6-7 NKJV)

Peace can therefore be provoked or triggered. We serve a God who is faithful to His words and respects principles defined in His words. Here God has clearly commanded us on how to harness His peace. Be anxious for nothing is God saying do not be anxious about ANYTHING. Your today's worry cannot solve tomorrow's problem, but focusing on God is the way to peace. If you are diligent to make your requests to God, worrying about nothing, through faith-inspired prayers, thanksgiving and supplication, this unspeakable peace will be yours.

Mary, the mother of Jesus, provides another notable example of provoked peace. Upon being informed by the angel Gabriel that she would bear the Messiah, her initial reaction was one of confusion and apprehension. Nevertheless, her obedient acceptance of God's would bring her to a place of peace. In Luke 1:38, she states, **"I am the Lord's servant,"** demonstrating her unwavering trust in God's plan.

Mary's situation illustrates that accepting situation beyond our control, even when difficult to understand, can lead to significant inner peace. Her life serves as an example for us to let go of anxieties and concerns, thus promoting a sense of serenity amidst life's uncertainties.

During Sermon on the Mount, Christ speaks:

"Therefore, I tell you, stop being perpetually uneasy (anxious and worried) about your life, what you shall eat or what you shall drink; or about your body, what you shall put on. Is not life greater [in quality] than food, and the body [far above and more excellent] than clothing? Look at the birds of the air; they neither sow nor reap nor gather into barns, and yet your heavenly Father keeps feeding them. Are you not worth much more than they? And who of you by worrying and being anxious can add one unit of measure (cubit) to his stature or to the span of his life? [Ps. 39:5-7.] But if God so clothes the grass of the field, which today is alive and green and tomorrow is tossed into the furnace, will He not much more surely clothe you, O you of little faith? So do not worry or be anxious about tomorrow, for tomorrow will have worries and anxieties of its own. Sufficient for each day is its own trouble." (Matthew 6:25-27, 30, 34 AMPC)

Christ's overall message in Philippians 4:6-7 is about a way that guarantees us peace, through:

- Prayer
- Supplication
- Thanksgiving
- Making your requests known to God

And the peace of God, which surpasses all understanding, will guard your hearts and minds through Christ Jesus.

This kind of peace, inferred from Peter's writing below:

"Therefore humble yourselves under the mighty hand of God, that He may exalt you in due time, casting all your care upon Him, for He cares for you. Be sober, be vigilant; because your

adversary the devil walks about like a roaring lion, seeking whom he may devour. Resist him, steadfast in the faith, knowing that the same sufferings are experienced by your brotherhood in the world. But [l]may the God of all grace, who called us to His eternal glory by Christ Jesus, after you have suffered a while, perfect, establish, strengthen, and settle *you.* To Him *be* the glory and the dominion forever and ever. Amen." (1 Peter 5:6-11 NKJV)

The promise to "perfect, establish, strengthen and settle you after one has suffered a while" is a flawless description of peace, for, without peace, none can be truly perfected, established, strengthened or settled.

Are you focused on the problem or the solution?

You can either choose to fix your mind on the problems and the challenges: your failures, the betrayals, your lean bank account, the rejection and others' behaviour and problems, or you can fix your mind on the problem solver - God, who gives you the ability, power and grace to contain and overcome whatever life, people and situations throw at you.

STEALERS OF INNER PEACE

These are the things that steal your inner peace contrary to the peace God has left and gifted to us. The list is inexhaustive and include:

- Ignorance of your identity and worth (Hosea 4:6)
- Greed and Lack of contentment
- Spirit of Covetousness
- Unhealthy Comparison

- Sins and transgression
- Lust and carnal thinking

ESSENTIALS FOR ACHIEVING INNER PEACE

- **IDENTIFY AND ACKKNOWLEDGE YOUR SPECIALNESS**

  This is about recognizing your unique identity as a creation of God and appreciating your special place in His plans.

  "**But you *are* a chosen generation, a royal priesthood, a holy nation, His own special people, that you may proclaim the praises of Him who called you out of darkness into His marvellous light."** (1 Peter 2:9).

  Depicting you as God's perfect creation the book of Deuteronomy writes:

  "He is the Rock; his deeds are perfect. Everything he does is just and fair. He is a faithful God who does no wrong; how just and upright he is!" (Deuteronomy 32:4).

  Therefore, acknowledging that you are a uniquely created being, which aligns with the concept of divine perfection, allows you to refute and align contrary thoughts that can steal your peace in accordance with this belief (2 Corinthians 10:5). This helps eliminate comparison mind-set that hinders joy and provides peace through assurance of God's perfect plans for man set forth as described in Jeremiah 29:11.

  "For I know the thoughts that I think toward you, says the Lord, thoughts of peace and not of evil, to give you a future and a hope."

- **BE CONTENT**

This aspect of contentment has to do with being satisfied and fulfilled with who you are and what God has made you to be rather than the satisfaction with your material possession, which is another aspect of contentment.

"Before I formed you in the womb I knew you; Before you were born, I sanctified you; I ordained you a prophet to the nations." (Jeremiah 1:5 NKJV)

- **BE GRATEFUL**

Gratitude is an expression of thankfulness and appreciation towards one's creator, stemming from a sense of contentment with one's identity and the unique gifts bestowed by God.

"I thank you, God for making me so mysteriously complex! Everything you do is marvellously breathtaking. It simply amazes me to think about it! How thoroughly you know me, Lord!" (Psalm 139:44 TPT)

Set aside time each day to recognize and acknowledge the small or minor things for which you are grateful. Concentrating on positive aspects of life can improve your inner peace and overall sense of well-being.

Practising this regularly can foster a sense of gratitude, which provides substantial benefits for your emotional well-being.

➢ DESIGNATE TIME FOR REST AND REFLECTION

This period of restful and prayerful separation from busyness, for a time of edifying of silence and solitude is important for refuelling, rejuvenation for advancement, and for our peace and well-being.

In periods of high stress or potential burnout at home, work, business, or ministry, it is useful to take a moment for self-reflection. Spend a few minutes being still, focusing on your breathing and the present moment. This practice can improve mental clarity and positively affect your overall well-being.

Jesus often withdrew to lonely places and prayed (Luke 5:16). In the sea of Galilea scenario for instance, we saw the humanity of rest-needing Jesus as he slept peacefully in the stern (Mark 4:35-39).

The Gospels frequently mention Jesus' solitude and silence. He began his ministry this way, made important decisions, and addressed emotions such as grief. This practice helped him manage the demands of his ministry and maintain his well-being. It was also how he instructed his disciples, prepared for significant ministry events, and readied himself for his death on the cross. This is evidence that rest is important for functioning, overall well-being, and inner peace.

➢ PRACTICE SELF-CARE AND POSITIVE FOCUS

It is easy to become ensnared in negative thoughts; however, it is essential to continually focus on the positive.

Deliberately seek out the silver linings and find satisfaction in even the smallest of God-created righteous pleasures. Every aspect of self-care covered under here, including mindfulness and self-awareness is important.

- **MINDFULNESS** is the practice of gently focusing your awareness on the present moment over and over, immersing oneself in the present moment, directing attention to focus (on the positive) and gently retraining the mind to settle into the present moment. It's kind of like becoming a parent to your mind rather than letting it control you. It is believed that practising mindfulness over and over with patience and compassion for yourself, can teach the mind to be still, for inner peace (Healthline.com).
- **SELF-AWARENESS** is our capacity to stand apart from ourselves and examine our thinking, our motives, our history, our scripts, our actions, and our habits and tendencies, involving deep personal honesty that comes from asking and answering hard questions (Stephen R. Covey, 2015).
  Embracing this practice facilitates the release of detrimental thoughts, creating space for gaining new insights and cherishing the abundant splendour and happiness in life.
- **SETTING REALISTIC EXPECTATION** is a form of self-care that guarantees you peace of the mind. Maintaining a realistic perspective while setting personal goals and expectations is essential. This approach helps to prevent disillusionment and allows you to focus on achievable objectives. Achieving each goal or target can enhance self-belief and promote a sense of peace and steadiness.

However, unmet or unrealistic expectations may lead to frustration, anxiety, and stress, which can sometimes negatively impact self-worth and peace of mind.

Harbouring realistic expectations, you can genuinely value your achievements, fostering an even deeper sense of serenity within.

- **POSITIVE SELF REFLECTION**

  Take time to reflect on your life and choices. This helps you understand yourself better and uncover your motivations. Engaging in regular self-reflection facilitates mental clarity and promotes a heightened and healthy sense of inner peace.

- **SELF-EMPATHY**

  Self-empathy involves treating oneself with the same empathy and understanding as one would extend to a close friend. It includes showing compassion towards oneself. In difficult situations, practise self-compassion by providing yourself with supportive and positive affirmations, and allowing room to learn from your mistakes.

SURROUND YOURSELF WITH HEALTHY INFLUENCES

Proverbs 27:17 states, **"Iron sharpens iron, so one man sharpens another."** When iron blades are rubbed together, they become sharper and more effective. Similarly, when individuals engage in each other's lives in mutual edification, growth and improvement occur. When we're living in healthy fellowship, we rely on one another and help one another.

The New Testament is replete with guidance on how believers should relate to influence one another. They are to do good to each other (Galatians 6:10), bear each other's burdens (Galatians 6:2), restore each other (Galatians 6:1; James 5:19-20), stir one another on to love and good deeds (Hebrews 10:24-25) and pursue peace and edify one another (Romans 14:19).

As iron sharpens iron in every area of life, so should one person sharpen another in pursuing things that make for peace.

It is imperative to deliberately associate with individuals who contribute to your personal journey and professional development. Interact with those who emphasize your strengths or offer constructive criticism in a supportive manner, aiding you in areas requiring improvement. By cultivating a network of supportive relationships, achieving inner peace and satisfaction becomes more feasible.

LIVING BY FAITH BUT CEDING CONTROL

James 2:26 writes:

"Just as the body is dead without breath, so also faith is dead without good works." Therefore, while we do what is within our control, it is important that we cede control to God, to determine the outcome, confident in the fact that if we ask anything according to His will, He will do it (1 John 5:14) and that if we delight in the Lord, in our ways and actions, He will give us our heart's desires (Psalm 37:5).

Learn to let go of control over every aspect of life. Prayerfully accept circumstances beyond your influence and control and focus on being present in each moment. By fostering acceptance and acknowledging the challenges of life as subject to divine knowledge and control, it is possible to achieve genuine peace and contentment. This inner peace will develop naturally.

Finding inner harmony is a lifelong journey that can start anytime. Finding inner peace is a personal journey that requires patience and trust in the Lord, consistent with the wisdom of Solomon in Proverbs 3:5-6 reflected below:

"Lean on, trust in, *and* be confident in the Lord with all your heart *and* mind and do not rely on your own insight *or* understanding. In all your ways know, recognize, *and* acknowledge Him, and He will direct *and* make straight *and* plain your paths." (Proverbs 3:5-6 AMPC)

From UCB Word for today on How to Have Peace, Trusting in the LORD:

> *"The Bible says, 'Trust in the Lord with all your heart, and lean not on your own understanding; in all your ways acknowledge Him, and He shall direct your paths' (vv. 5-6 NKJV). God wants you to trust Him. As long as you're struggling to figure things out on your own, you're not trusting God and you won't have peace. You must trust Him with your health, your money, your relationships, and your future. Everything! God never makes a mistake. All that happens in your life fits into His plan for you – even the problems and miseries and troubles you bring on yourself. He fits everything flawlessly into His plan for you (see Romans 8:28). And all He expects from you is to trust Him instead of attempting to figure everything out – that you acknowledge He is in control. When you do this, He promises to 'make your paths straight' (Proverbs 3:6 NIV). When we aim at directing our own lives, we follow arbitrary paths filled with indecisiveness: 'Should I do this or that? Should I go here or over there?' And it produces stress! But as soon as you trust in the Lord, He directs your paths and makes them successful, not stressful. 'Do not be anxious about anything, but in every situation, by prayer and petition, with thanksgiving, present*

> *your requests to God. And the peace of God, which transcends all understanding, will guard your hearts and your minds' (Philippians 4:6-7 NIV). Note the order – prayer first, then peace. So if you're not praying, you're probably worrying. And worry is a worthless emotion – a waste! So when pressure starts accumulating, instead of panicking, start praying! Prayer is a remarkable stress reliever."*

By embracing our identity (in Christ), contentment with attitude of gratitude, establishing practical expectations, engaging in introspection, prioritizing self-care, and surrounding oneself with positive influences, one can gradually construct a resilient groundwork for inner serenity.

Since the individuals and entities you allow access to your life, mind and thoughts through relationships and connections play a significant role in your well-being and development, the next chapter discusses peace with others and interpersonal relationships.

Chapter 8

INTERPERSONAL RELATIONSHIPS - PEACE WITH MAN

"If possible, as far as it depends on you, live at peace with everyone." (Romans 12:18 AMP)

Human beings are creations of God, made in His image and likeness. Humans possess inherent goodness and are endowed with dominion, capability, and the capacity to live harmoniously with others. Achieving peace requires us to actively address human complexities in ways that foster mutual understanding, justice, and enduring harmony.

The writer of Hebrews then added:

"Work at living in peace with everyone, and work at living a holy life, for those who are not holy will not see the Lord." (Hebrews 12:14 NLT).

Achieving peace with others involves intentionally developing harmonious relationships based on empathy. It requires an appropriate level of affection towards individuals, considering their well-being, engaging with them as fellow human beings, and treating them with respect and consideration, in the manner you would wish to be treated.

According to Jon Gordon: ***"The best legacy you could leave is not some building that is named after you or a piece of jewellery but rather a world that has been impacted and touched by your presence, your joy, and your positive actions."***

This wisdom clearly suggests that there are works to do for people to live in peace with others.

Then Dale Carnegie wrote:

"When dealing with people, let us remember we are not dealing with creatures of logic. We are dealing with creatures of emotion, creatures bristling with prejudices and motivated by pride and vanity."

Peace with man therefore does not come from our passivity, our reluctance to act (seek it) and / or our indifference. Peace with others is a product of who you are and what you do (with who you are or influences around you).

Leadership expert John Maxwell says, ***"You'll never change your life until you change something you do daily because the secret of your success is found in your daily routine."*** According to John Maxwell's insightful perspective here, a person's destiny is influenced by their capacity to develop and maintain empowering relationships with both God and fellow humans, for the benefit of all.

Your daily actions reflect who you are, shaped by both nature and nurture.

YOUR NATURE & PEACE

About our body and its control Apostle Paul in 1 Corinthians 6:19-20 (AMPC) writes:

"Do you not know that your body is the temple (the very sanctuary) of the Holy Spirit Who lives within you, Whom you have received [as a Gift] from God? You are not your own, You were bought with a price [purchased with a [preciousness and paid for, [made His own]. So then, honour God *and* bring glory to Him in your body."

Your peaceful nature is foundationally determined and controlled by the spirit of God that lives in you, giving you enduring ability to manifest the fruits of the spirit that includes peace:

"But the Holy Spirit produces this kind of fruit in our lives: love, joy, peace, patience, kindness, goodness, faithfulness, gentleness, and self-control. There is no law against these things!" (Galatians 5:22-23 NLT)

You cannot give what you don't have. It's the Holy-Spirit-produced peace in you that overflows into others' lives. By aligning your actions with the guidance and direction of the spirit that lives within you, you will achieve inner peace that means you can positively influence those you interact with.

YOUR NURTURE & PEACE

Nurture in this context refers to all the outside influences that sway and shape a person's behaviour (Psychology Central).

Nurture pertains to the influences of our upbringing, the education and training we receive, and the environment in which we are raised. These factors collectively shape our lives, fostering a mindset that promotes peace in both our thoughts and actions.

Of all the nurture factors that help to shape one's life for peace, parental style alongside educational, social cultural and faith environments are key. These are environments where individuals are raised and mentored during the formative stages of their lives. These environments influence beliefs and thinking, which determine how things are perceived, analysed, and how emotions are created and reactions to events are formed.

MINDSETS AND PEACE

Discussing the variations among individuals that might explain why some experience panic and a lack of peace while others stay calm in challenging situations, Carol Dweck states:

"Since the dawn of time, people have thought differently, acted differently, and fared differently from each other..." Today most experts agree it's not either - or. It's not nature or nurture, genes or environment. From conception on, there's a constant give-and-take between the two...For thirty years, my research has shown that the view (belief) you adopt for yourself profoundly affect the way you lead your life... Believing that your qualities are carved in stone - the fixed mindset - creates an urgency to prove yourself over and over...There is another - the growth mindset based on the belief that your basic qualities are things that you can cultivate through your effort, your strategies, and help from others. Although people may differ in every which way - in their initial talent and aptitudes, interests or temperaments - everyone can change and grow through application and experience...To give you a better view of how the two mindsets work (that might determine your peace or otherwise), imagine - as vividly as you can - that you are a young adult having a really bad day: One day, you go to a class that is really important to you and that you like a lot. The professor returns the mid-term paper to the class. You got a C+. You're very disappointed. That evening on the

way back to your home, you find that you've gotten a parking ticket. Being really frustrated, you call your best friend to share your experience but are sort of brushed off. What would you think? What would you feel? What would you do? When I asked people with the fixed mindset, this is what they said: "I'd feel like a reject," "I'm a total failure." I am an idiot." I'm a lose." I'd feel worthless and dumb - everyone's better than me." "I'm slime." In other words, they'd see what happened as a direct measure of their competence and worth (to the detriment of their peace). This is what they'd think about their lives. "My life is pitiful." "I have no life'" "Somebody upstairs doesn't like me." "The world is out to get me." "Someone is out to destroy me." "Nobody loves me, everybody hates me'" "Life is unfair and all efforts are useless." "Life stinks." "I'm stupid. Nothing good ever happens to me." "I'm most unlucky person on this earth." Excuse me, was there death and destruction or just a grade, a ticket, and a bad phone call? Are these just people with low self-esteem? Or card-carrying pessimist? No... What is there to do? So how would they cope? "I would not bother put so much time and effort into doing well in anything." "Do nothing." (Remember) it was a mid-term not a final. It was a parking ticket not a car wreck. They were "sort of brushed off" not rejected outright. Nothing catastrophic happened. <u>Yet from this raw material the fixed mindset created the feeling of utter failure and paralysis,</u>

When I gave people with growth mindset the same vignette, here's what they said. They'd think: "I need to try harder in class, be more careful when parking the car, and wonder if my friend (who brushed me off) was having a bad day." The C+ would tell me that I'd have to work a lot harder in the class, but I have the semester to pull up my grade." (Carol Dweck, Mindset 2017)

Based on Carol Dweck's research findings (which you can find in her book called MINDSET):

- Someone with a growth mindset views intelligence, abilities, and talents as learnable and capable of improvement through effort. On the other hand, someone with a fixed mindset views those same traits as inherently stable and unchangeable over time.
- A growth mindset allows you to believe in the potential for improvement; it makes relationships feel a bit easier and success seem within reach. With a growth mindset, you will learn to look at conflict as an opportunity for improvement – both for yourselves and the relationship.
- A fixed mindset makes you feel limited to what you already have, and makes you feel dependent on others to make you feel good. It holds you back from success because you're afraid of failure.

Fixed Mindset Individuals:

- Seek collaborators who hold them in high regard.
- Expect constant admiration and adoration.
- Find difficulty in accepting criticism or suggestions for improvement.
- Prioritize stability and consistent dynamics.

Growth Mindset Individuals:

- Seek collaborators who acknowledge their shortcomings and are committed to personal growth.
- Value feedback that promotes personal growth and development.
- Excel in relationships where communication is transparent and mutual learning is prioritized.
- Aim for a partnership that fosters growth and evolution

WHY GROWTH MINDSET IS IMPORTANT FOR PEACE

Individuals with a fixed mindset may face difficulties in developing dynamic relationships or effectively navigating challenging relational experiences, particularly during conflicts, crucial conversations, or situations requiring changes or adaptive responses.

For Examples:

"Because people with fixed mindset have no recipe for healing, when they are hurt, all they would like to do is hurt back in return." - Carol DWECK

"For people with growth mindset, number one goal is forgiveness, and for those with fixed mindset, their recipe for "healing" is revenge." - Carol DWECK

"A good, lasting relationship is not automatic. It comes through effort and working through inevitable differences." - Carol DWECK

"When people with fixed mindset see flaws in their partner, they become contemptuous of the relationship and give up, but when people with growth mindset see one, they work on it and believe they can have fine relationship." - Carol DWECK

"People with fixed mindset blind themselves to flaws in their relationship or partner so they don't have to go that route (hoping it will go away or that there is nothing they can do) but for Growth-minded people, they face with optimism and fix it." - Carol DWECK

How To Build A Growth Mindset For Peace In Relationships

- Embrace Challenges that strengthen relationship including crucial conversations.
- View challenges as opportunities rather than obstacles. Each challenge represents a chance for learning and growth, rather than a barrier to achieving success.
- Recognise Effort, Not Just Achievement.
- Focus on praising effort, not just outcomes. Consistent effort leads to mastery.
- Celebrate small victories and progress toward larger goals.
- Emphasize Learning Rather Than Seeking Approval.
- Concentrate on gaining knowledge from every situation instead of seeking validation from others. This change in perspective diminishes the fear of judgment and empowers you to pursue more ambitious goals.
- Surround Yourself with Growth-Minded People as their attitudes and behaviours can provide examples for you to follow. Interacting with individuals who support and stimulate your progress can enhance your development.
- Prioritise empathy and serve one another.

Entitlement and retaliation are not good partners, but communication is their friend. Serve one another with love, work for healing and forgive for peace.

CREATIVE ORDER AND HUMAN CONDITION

The story of creation beautifully demonstrates God, not just as God of order but as the author of peace. Genesis chapter 1 presents God as a loving creator who brings order and goodness into existence.

Unfortunately, God's original plan for a peaceful world which Eden represented was punctured by sin that robbed man of God's intended order and peace. The inevitable outcome of man's failing is some elements of human condition, including trials, tribulations, wars and disorder.

"These things I have spoken to you, that in Me you may have peace. In the world you will have tribulation; but be of good cheer, I have overcome the world." (John 16:33 NKJV)

This passage highlights the certainty of tribulations and underscores the essential need for peace.

PEACE IS SHARED AND WISDOM IS NEEDED

A life of peace is never achieved in isolation.

True peace is developed through our interactions with others—men and women, young and old—in communities composed of individuals with diverse personalities, temperaments, emotions, and agendas. It is encountered in experiences that challenge us and within various settings where human interaction occurs, including our homes, workplaces, public spaces, and broader environments. Consequently, ensuring a life of genuine peace necessitates the deliberate cultivation of a lifestyle that fosters positive and successful living, thereby positively influencing oneself and others within our environments and relationships.

In a world where offence from others is inevitable and where war, injustice, and inevitable trials occur, it is important to manage what is within our control. This involves taking responsibility for our actions, managing our own affairs, and responding to situations beyond our control with care, grace, and wisdom.

Here again is Dale Carnegie's wisdom:

"When dealing with people, let us remember we are not dealing with creatures of logic. We are dealing with creatures of emotion, creatures bristling with prejudices and motivated by pride and vanity."

Wisdom is needed to deal with humans and their complexities for peace. This wisdom from above guarantees peace in addition to other virtues that make peace an assured outcome.

"But the wisdom from above is always pure, filled with peace, considerate and teachable. It is filled with love and never displays prejudice or hypocrisy in any form and it always bears the beautiful harvest of righteousness! Good seeds of wisdom's fruit will be planted with peaceful acts by those who cherish making peace." (James 3:17-18 TPT)

- Wisdom allows you to perceive and understand the experiences and challenges of others, enabling you to provide compassion and support for a peaceful life (Romans 12:15).
- Wisdom with understanding, helps us to navigate life's challenges with grace and discernment.
- To have peace with man we must know or learn how to deal with difficult people at one time or another.
- A difficult person may be volatile, rash, rude, disrespectful, belligerent, selfish, unloving, argumentative, unkind, bullish, abusive or simply annoying. It could be in an office, at home, at a cafe, in the bus or at a cinema. Unfortunately, they may not know they are difficult due to lack of insight or foundational issues that have to do with their background or nurture. They cause difficulties and disturb or steal your peace through their actions or inactions, words or silence and/or by breaching boundaries.

- **Dealing with difficult people for peace therefore becomes an exercise in self-control and patience, in appropriately redefining boundaries, telling yourself stories that edify, and in responding to the triggers with wisdom, grace and love.**

PEACE AND PATH TO HUMAN ACTION

According to Patterson et al in the book "*Crucial Conversation*", human actions stem from what we SEE or HEAR, which shapes the STORY we tell ourselves, leading to our EMOTIONS and ultimately dictating our ACTIONS.

Patterson et al (2021) described the sequence of events and internal processes that lead to a specific action or decision, starting with OBSERVATION (of what others do), followed by INTERPRETATIONS (based on what was seen or heard), then feelings (triggered by those interpretations), and finally, actions (informed by the emotions).

This explains why two people can perceive the same event but respond differently.

Patterson et al further submit that stories matter because they create feelings. Just after we observe what others do and just before we feel some EMOTIONS about it, we tell ourselves a STORY or STORIES. We add meaning to the action we observed. We make a guess at the motive driving the behaviour. We call this our Path to Action because it explains how emotions, thoughts, and experiences lead to our actions. If you can therefore control the narrative and the story you tell yourself, bereft of mistrust, but based on love for others, your actions will be controlled and in keeping with peace.

Since peace denotes a state of calmness, tranquillity, or quietude—emotions comparable to joy or sadness—we can assert that Patterson's approach to **Emotion & Action** at the human level offers an explanation of how our reactions, particularly to negative behaviours, are essential for maintaining peace in interpersonal relationships.

When individuals adopt a growth mindset, it positively influences their stories and their ability to respond appropriately and lovingly to human behaviour and offence, fostering inner peace and harmonious relationship with others.

According to Patterson et al, **Three Clever Stories We Tell Ourselves** (Adapted from Crucial conversation by Patterson et al)

Have you ever told a story and left out key details to the listeners? People may tell different versions of a story to avoid responsibility or to portray themselves in a positive light. These revised stories can omit important details and adjust the narrative to fit specific needs, meaning that we have an outcome that could be peace or the absence of it. We often rationalize our actions through clever narratives that justify behaviours which may damage our relationships and outcomes.

There are three primary types of stories we tell ourselves to feel justified in such actions. To effectively counter these narratives, it is crucial to **consider the entirety of the situation**.

1. **Victim Stories: "It's not my fault."**

   We tell ourselves we are not contributing to the problem.

   For example, you forget to complete an important task for the boss who just returned from a business trip and react by saying, "I didn't have the help or time that I needed to complete the project on time." You are telling yourself that you are being punished for the company's lack of resources and talent.

Tell the Rest of the Story: Turn yourself from a victim into a contributor. Ask yourself: What am I pretending not to notice about my role in the problem?

2. Villain Stories: "It's your fault."

These stories overemphasize others' nasty qualities or perceived incompetence and are often accompanied with labelling.

For example, we may find ourselves saying, "Of course I yelled at him. Didn't you see what he did? He deserved it." When we turn human beings into villains, we feel justified in insulting or abusing them.

Tell the Rest of the Story: Turn others from villains into humans. Ask yourself: Why would a reasonable, rational, decent person do this?

3. Helpless Stories: "There's nothing I can do."

Here we convince ourselves that there are no healthy options for taking action and we can't change our situation.

For example, you find yourself talking with a colleague about an idea for a new operations process but say, "If I presented this to the leaders they would probably just get defensive like they always do—I'm not going to say anything!" Or on the flip side, "If I didn't yell, then the work wouldn't get done. What choice do I have!"

> **Tell the Rest of the Story**: Turn yourself from helpless to able. Ask yourself: "What should I do right now to move toward what I really want?"

Challenging our stories with questions allows us to uncover important information so that our stories better represent reality, and this helps us engage in better dialogues that promote peace when we find ourselves in a crucial conversation.

THE LESSON AND PEACE MESSAGE FROM HERE

- Stories matter.
- What we hear influences the stories we tell ourselves, which in turn affect our feelings and emotions, ultimately guiding our actions or responses.
- The action or response could be war or peace
- Story told or interpretation given can be truth or falsity
- Story told or the interpretation given could be the difference between peace and war
- If you want peace tell the story as it is or seek for clarity to understand if what you heard, or your interpretation does not point to peace.
- Overall, no matter what comes between Story and Emotions, always respond with grace and peace

The next chapter will look at the foundation as an important nurture factor in determining the peace of the family and the society at large.

Chapter 9

IT ALL STARTS WITH FOUNDATION

"There is no doubt that it is around the family and the home that all the greatest virtues, the most dominating virtues of human, are created, strengthened and maintained."
- Winston Churchill

The foundation of society is the family unit, which typically consists of parents and their child or children. For those awaiting the blessing of offspring, family or home refers to the partnership between husband and wife.

Families serve as essential units in raising children to become adults who contribute to society. Just as individuals are influenced by their environments, society is also shaped by these influences. Maintaining peace within homes and families is critical for social stability and the overall well-being of individuals and communities worldwide. Therefore, promoting a culture of peace can create an environment where everyone can prosper and lead productive lives.

For a truly peaceful home, harmonious family relationships are required:

- between the couple
- between each parent and the children.
- between (or among) the children.
- And between each member of the family and the world outside the home.

Given that conflicts within family relationships or between family members and external parties can affect the entire family unit, it is crucial to foster a culture of peace within the family. Such a culture is vital for maintaining harmony and stability both internally and in their interactions with others and the broader community.

For a family to achieve peace, it is essential that relationships are harmonious across various experiences and settings. The sustainability of peace is contingent upon cultivating a robust foundation within the family, wherein each member embraces values that embody virtue. These values should be instilled both in domestic settings and throughout the broader community, serving to enhance their lives and positively impact the world.

Personal and family values can be viewed as a system that is important for consistently achieving favourable outcomes in difficult situations. Often, intentions do not lead to results because of the absence of an internal system for execution. Personal and family values provide this essential framework.

In his book LEGACY, James Kerr details on how a New Zealand Team, the All Blacks instituted and nurtured peak performance and sustained a high-performance culture. The core idea of James Kerr's "Legacy" is that focusing on building high operating standards and developing sound and foundational character in people, group or players, and fostering a strong team culture will naturally lead to success, as the "score takes care of itself." By creating an environment within your family, workplace, personal space, and boundaries where virtue, high-performance behaviour, and peace are normalized, you will effectively manage your temperament and enhance your quality of life. In a professional setting, this approach will optimize the capabilities of your team members, leading to the success and growth of your business or enterprise.

Unfortunately, our peace will be tried by inevitable moments of pressure, trials or troubles, and John 16:33 captures this:

"And everything I've taught you is so that the peace which is in me will be in you and will give you great confidence as you rest in me. For in this unbelieving world you will experience trouble and sorrows, but you must be courageous, for I have conquered the world!" (John 16:33 TPT)

PEACE AND PRESSURES

Pressure can be a good thing if it's taken as a catalyst for change, but pressure can undermine peace when we give in to its negative impact.

Mistakes can occur under pressure, which may impact the human mind and potentially lead to panic if not managed properly.

Bad decisions including ones that affect your peace, James Kerr argues, "are not made through lack of skills or innate judgement: they are made because of inability to handle pressure at the pivotal moment. "It's suggested in LEGACY that Under pressure, unfortunately it is the thinking that shots down and you are relying on instinct and emotion - which means you are at big risk of bad behaviour. Once the thinking is compromised, you lose focus on the process, and this means you are cut up in the outcomes which inevitably include lack of peace

Finding inner peace is important for maintaining tranquillity and a sense of calm in challenging times in a world of pressure, trials, demands and adversities.

If therefore you create a value system that puts your emotions in check in response to inevitable stimuli and pressures around you, you are then better placed for multidimensional peace.

VALUES AND LESSON FROM STORY OF THE RECHABITES

The story of the Obedient Rechabites below presents an example of values.

"The word which came to Jeremiah from the Lord in the days of Jehoiakim the son of Josiah, king of Judah, saying, [2] "Go to the house of the Rechabites, speak to them, and bring them into the house of the Lord, into one of the chambers, and give them wine to drink."

[3] Then I took Jaazaniah the son of Jeremiah, the son of Habazziniah, his brothers and all his sons, and the whole house of the Rechabites, [4] and I brought them into the house of the Lord, into the chamber of the sons of Hanan the son of Igdaliah, a man of God, which *was* by the chamber of the princes, above the chamber of Maaseiah the son of Shallum, the keeper of the [a]door. [5] Then I set before the sons of the house of the Rechabites bowls full of wine, and cups; and I said to them, "Drink wine."

[6] But they said, "We will drink no wine, for Jonadab the son of Rechab, our father, commanded us, saying, 'You shall drink no wine, you nor your sons, forever. [7] You shall not build a house,

sow seed, plant a vineyard, nor have *any of these;* but all your
days you shall dwell in tents, that you may live many days in
the land where you are sojourners.' 8 Thus we have obeyed the
voice of Jonadab the son of Rechab, our father, in all that he
charged us, to drink no wine all our days, we, our wives, our
sons, or our daughters, 9 nor to build ourselves houses to dwell
in; nor do we have vineyard, field, or seed. 10 But we have dwelt
in tents and have obeyed and done according to all that Jonadab
our father commanded us. 11 But it came to pass, when
Nebuchadnezzar king of Babylon came up into the land, that we
said, 'Come, let us go to Jerusalem for fear of the army of the
Chaldeans and for fear of the army of the Syrians.' So we dwell
at Jerusalem."

12 Then came the word of the Lord to Jeremiah, saying, 13 "Thus
says the Lord of hosts, the God of Israel: 'Go and tell the men of
Judah and the inhabitants of Jerusalem, "Will you not receive
instruction to obey My words?" says the Lord. 14 "The words of
Jonadab the son of Rechab, which he commanded his sons, not
to drink wine, are performed; for to this day they drink none,
and obey their father's commandment. But although I have
spoken to you, rising early and speaking, you did not [c]obey
Me. 15 I have also sent to you all My servants the prophets, rising
up early and sending *them,* saying, 'Turn now everyone from
his evil way, amend your doings, and do not go after other gods
to serve them; then you will dwell in the land which I have
given you and your fathers.' But you have not inclined your ear,
nor obeyed Me. 16 Surely the sons of Jonadab the son of Rechab
have performed the commandment of their father, which he
commanded them, but this people has not obeyed Me."'

17 "Therefore thus says the Lord God of hosts, the God of Israel:
'Behold, I will bring on Judah and on all the inhabitants of
Jerusalem all the doom that I have pronounced against

them; because I have spoken to them but they have not heard, and I have called to them but they have not answered.'"

18 And Jeremiah said to the house of the Rechabites, "Thus says the Lord of hosts, the God of Israel: 'Because you have obeyed the commandment of Jonadab your father, and kept all his precepts and done according to all that he commanded you, 19 therefore thus says the Lord of hosts, the God of Israel: "Jonadab the son of Rechab shall not lack a man to stand before Me forever." (Jeremiah 35:1-19 NKJV).

The main issue here was not wine consumption but following their leader Jonadab's instruction. Jeremiah used this to highlight the importance of values and obedience. A second contrast was evident in the way that the Rechabites obeyed the command of their father, while the people of Judah and Jerusalem disobeyed the commands of God Himself, though He repeatedly brought those commands to them through His prophets. Obedience was the primary focus, rather than commenting specifically on the consumption of wine. Nonetheless, **God acknowledged the Rechabites** for their steadfast commitment to abstaining from alcohol, despite the temptation to do otherwise.

Just as the Rechabites were raised with this value in their homes, consider the potential impact on the world if our families were founded on temperance, mutual respect, love, kindness, gentleness, and other values that promote peace. This is precisely what we are all called to instil in our homes. When life in homes is based on a culture of peace, it will have positive effects on communities, workplaces, and social environments.

A STRONG FOUNDATION IS THEREFORE ESSENTIAL

Building a home with Godly foundation guarantees you this peace even when the storms of life strike.

Matthew 7:24-27 outlines the characteristics of such a family:

""Everyone who hears my teaching and applies it to his life can be compared to a wise man who built his house on an unshakable foundation. When the rains fell and the flood came, with fierce winds beating upon his house, it stood firm because of its strong foundation. "But everyone who hears my teaching and does not apply it to his life can be compared to a foolish man who built his house on sand. When it rained and rained and the flood came, with wind and waves beating upon his house, it collapsed and was swept away."" (Matthew 7:24-27 TPT)

When each family member is first committed to God, the author of peace, it results in the transformation of their minds towards seeking peace. Consequently, every individual becomes a beacon of light in their workplace, social environments, and communities.

The book of Matthew writes about such person or persons as light:

14 "You are the light of the world—like a city on a hilltop that cannot be hidden. 15 No one lights a lamp and then puts it under a basket. Instead, a lamp is placed on a stand, where it gives light to everyone in the house. 16 In the same way, let your good deeds shine out for all to see, so that everyone will praise your heavenly Father." (Matthew 5:14-16)

.... and we see the light shine in Chapter 10.

Chapter 10

YOUR LIGHT SHINES WHEREVER YOU GO

"If there is righteousness in the heart, there will be beauty in the character. If there is beauty in the character, there will be harmony in our home. If there is harmony in the home, there will be order in the nations. When there is order in the nations, there will peace in the world."

— Confucius

Apart from time spent at home, the next greater percentage of our time is spent in our places of work.

It's estimated that the average adult living in the United States will spend 90,000 hours – or one-third of their lives – at work (Harvard Division of continuing education November 28, 2023).

This clearly shows that we spend a large percentage of our time in office. British workers for example will spend an average of 3,515 full days at work over the course of their lifetime. Workplace therefore matters, and so does what happens in our places of work. Positive workplace experiences enhance our well-being, while negative workplace experiences can disrupt one's peace and be detrimental to one's health.

Poor workplace culture can negatively impact a person's wellbeing but people working in companies with positive corporate culture are healthier, happier, more productive, and less likely to leave (Harvard Division of continuing education November 28, 2023).

Anxiety is workplace emotions that can kill one's peace if uncontrolled.

According to COMPSYCH Corporation (March 26, 2024) the world's largest provider of mental health services and GuidanceResources® for life, workplace anxiety stands as the primary challenge facing today's employees, surpassing other concerns such as depression, stress, and relationship issues. Their 2023 finding based on a representative sample analysis of more than 300,000 U.S. cases facilitated by ComPsych showed that a year before, nearly a quarter of people (24%) who reached out for mental health assistance did so to get help with anxiety. Their analysis underscores prevalence of workplace anxiety as the most significant mental health issue among U.S. workers.

Similarly, a ComPsych (2023) analysis of several thousand cases from its 2023 UK book of business found that nearly a third (31%) of the people who sought mental health assistance in the UK did so to get help with anxiety. This benchmark is seven percentage points higher than that seen in America, where anxiety was also the top presenting issue in 24% of U.S. cases.

As the number one presenting issue among UK workers, anxiety ranks higher than depression, stress, anger, occupational challenges, family issues, addiction, partner or relationship issues, and grief, among other areas people seek help with. While anxiety is not new to the British workforce – it's been the top presenting issue across the UK since 2019 – it did increase by more than a third (35%) from 2019 to 2023.

Ideally, our workplace should feel like a second home. This can be achieved by establishing rules and regulations, guidelines for standard professional behaviour, and clear boundaries. Adhering to these principles ensures a peaceful and harmonious working environment for everyone.

Various factors can impact one's peace in the workplace if there is a lack of self-awareness regarding work circumstances and no effort is made to maintain harmony with oneself, the work environment, and colleagues.

WORKPLACE STEALERS OF PEACE CAN BE:

(These are just a few examples as the list is not exhaustive)

A) Settings-related

These encompass, but are not limited to, institutional frameworks within your workplace, the environment, the ambience of the location, the organisational practices, workplace values, and structural hierarchies. They are not directly under your control. Examples are:

- Toxic work environment
- Unhygienic environment

Here you must find a way to be at peace with yourself and do all within your powers to keep the environment hygienic and the workplace healthy as much as lies within your powers. Changing the workplace starts with changing yourself.

B) Self-related

Here we have your way of life, your way of thinking and reasoning, and your way of doing things, which, although personal to you, can impact both your own life and others', including in the workplace.

Under here, also lies your experiences and exposures, your skills and abilities, which when productively harnessed, make you feel confident, secure and in a good place of peace

Examples are:

- Time management.
- Task management.

You can manage these factors to benefit yourself and improve the workplace for everyone, by being punctual and managing your time well, with effective prioritisation and completion of tasks.

C) Others - related

The complexity of peace lies in the fact that what others do matter: the actions or inaction of others go a very long way in determining the atmosphere and peace of a place and persons. No one lives good life in isolation and injury to one could be injury to all.

Examples are:

- Unfriendly colleague
- Challenges with a mentor

You can manage this by starting with yourself. Always be professional and treat everyone with respect and avoid discrimination.

I recall a workplace situation where as a new staff member in one of the hospitals I worked, an outgoing colleague warned me regarding a particular staff to be careful about, who was described as difficult and not a good team player. The intention was I, believe, to protect me from getting into trouble. This affected my peace a couple of weeks into the job, ruminating on this advice toward the staff, but I remained true to my conviction to relate with everyone with open mind, without any form of prejudice.

Six months down the line, I found the staff I was warned about to be both pleasant to work with and very professional. This was a big lesson in avoiding any form of workplace bias, prejudice or profiling, and in fact anything with potential to take my peace. Imagine if heeded the advice, the possibility of fighting another person's battle and undermining myself and taking a step that's contrary to the virtue of love and good neighbourliness.

The best way to guarantee you have a nice workplace colleague is to be one.

Friendly colleagues are likely to be sociable with appropriate smile and cheerful countenance that lightens your day. If that colleague is a mentor, a productive mentor-mentee relationship can improve workplace interactions and peace of the mind.

Constructive feedback is another important peace factor. Feedback is an essential tool for assessing the quality of your work. It also presents a remarkable quality improvement opportunity. Constructive feedback that gives you ideas for improvement can transform your career into a high performing experience and your day, into a very productive, happy, cheerful and peaceful one.

Attitude of gratitude and recognition inspires positive relationship. A culture of gratitude and recognition makes a colleague (in fact anyone) feel valued, fostering workplace happiness and peace. Appreciating others whether for their help or kindness, hard work or positive attitude, fosters a supportive and positive work environment. This can be as simple as a thank you note, a shout-out during a team meeting, or a recognition program that highlights outstanding contributions.

BEING AN ARCHITECT OF YOUR PEACE

Establishing a positive work-life balance is crucial for supporting overall well-being. It is essential to maintain a clear distinction between work responsibilities and personal life to ensure mental and emotional stability. Although it may not be within one's power to manage all external factors that can affect peace of mind, it is possible to manage those within one's control effectively.

The ability to adapt to change and embrace growth opportunities is vital for maintaining peace. This is wisdom and maturity.

The ability to find peace by managing stressors and utilizing peace-enhancing strategies directly or indirectly related to your work or daily family life is crucial for maintaining or increasing personal tranquillity, whether you are at home or away. The following chapter will examine various factors that contribute to a peaceful state of mind. It will address aspects that we may consider essential as well as those that may initially seem insignificant but ultimately impact our overall sense of peace, particularly when minor issues accumulate over time into significant challenges that disrupt tranquillity.

Chapter 11

LITTLE AND BIG PEACE BOOSTERS

"It's not the big things that add up in the end; it's the hundreds, thousands, or millions of little things that separate the ordinary from the extraordinary."

- Darren Hardy

The concept of "little peace boosters" and "big peace boosters" comes from the notion that individuals are the architects of their own destinies. This idea is coupled with the observation that humans naturally tend to focus on what they believe to be significant matters while often overlooking smaller ones, which can result in unintended consequences. Achieving peace across multiple dimensions requires attention to every detail, regardless of its size or perceived importance.

Robert Fulghum writes: ***"Peace is not something you wish for, it is something you make, something you are, something you do and something you give away."***

Big things or big decisions include who to marry, where to settle with one's family, one's career and other life-defining human choices. Small-sounding decisions by the day may include routine exercise, what to eat, what to wear and what time to attend a community event. Over time, what to eat for instance becomes increasingly significant, yielding positive or negative outcomes. For individuals maintaining healthy eating and exercise habits, these decisions can lead to beneficial results such as optimal weight, balanced cholesterol levels, and robust heart health, ultimately transforming their lives profoundly. On the contrary, day-by-day, unhealthy dietary choices overtime, will have amounted to a big, bad decision should such individual develop diabetes as a result.

In health, again, for instance, while avoiding unhealthy sexual behaviour is likely to protect one from contracting serious diseases like Hepatitis and HIV (which in complicated form is a potentially life-threatening condition) in a bid to live long in peace, unhealthy use of alcohol may kill sooner, from liver complications, and obesity from unhealthy dietary choices may result in quicker death from heart attack or stroke, and in medium to long term, death from cancer.

On the other hand, a faithful man or woman not involved in sinful act of adultery may lose his or her job and consequently peace, through habitual pattern of late coming at workplace, and a nice man who does not walk in the company of evil or murderous men, may end up in prison due to loose talk, gossip or fall out from momentary anger.

In the scenarios described above, what appeared to be "small things" eventually mattered most with life-defining consequences. Every decision matters and while one "big decision" may be all that's needed to trigger life-defining outcome, small decisions are often what compound to cause adverse events or experiences in our lives.

So it is for peace. While an individual may pursue a big decision of keeping a distance from others outside his or her home for various reasons, such as maintaining personal space, it may be a child in the house who has not received adequate and simple day-to-day care and nurturing time from their parents, that causes disruptions and loss of peace within the family, due to external influences or delinquent behaviour.

Similarly, an executive director, who is meticulous and professional in their role, making significant decisions and enjoying their time at the office, may find their peace disrupted by a driving offence caused by a simple and momentary period of distraction.

I recall parking-related charge I got when I worked in a Manchester hospital, which I contested. I made payment which I was told was wrongly directed. My initial appeals were rejected. Due to delays in addressing an offer of early payment, or taking the matter to court, I missed the deadline for action. The attempt to contest what I recognized as an incorrect ticket was unsuccessful due to delays caused by procrastination. This was an event that affected my time, financial resources, and my peace during the period it lasted, which was over a decade ago.

I also recall a time I got a driving ticket because I was doing 35 miles per hour or so, in 30 miles an hour road. This was during our month of fasting and praying which I strictly observed. I was sad that I got this ticket which made me lose my peace that period and it made me wonder why God would allow me to get a driving ticket during a period of spiritual exercise, which on reflection, clearly appears to be a reaction not borne out of discernment. The speed ticket I got should have nothing to do with God; it was justice for unintentional bad driving behaviour, with matching disciplinary penalty by the authority, which according to Romans 13:4-6 is an agent of God for our good:

"The authorities are God's servants, sent for your good. But if you are doing wrong, of course you should be afraid, for they have the power to punish you. They are God's servants, sent for the very purpose of punishing those who do what is wrong. So you must submit to them, not only to avoid punishment, but also to keep a clear conscience."

Multidimensional peace therefore requires maintaining focus and adhering to principles in family, personal life, and the workplace. It involves following the law and fulfilling the responsibilities of citizenship. It also involves attending to minor details and decisions, ensuring that nothing requiring our attention or action is overlooked. Additionally, when expectations are not met or a mistake is made, it is important to take responsibility and be honest with the truth which can set free (John 8:32) and provide relief with mental peace.

LITTLE PEACE BOOSTERS

Every decision has significance, and indecision can cause problems. The small decisions made regularly, such as what to wear, what to eat, or when to wake up, cumulatively create substantial impacts. When these minor decisions relate to important aspects of life, their cumulative effects can significantly influence life outcomes.

Small, seemingly insignificant decisions and our daily choices can remarkably affect our sense of peace, impacting activities from daily routines to overall mental health.

GOOD SLEEP HYGIENE

Relaxing bedtime ritual with timely waking is healthy. Structured bedtime practices such as taking a warm bath, reading a book, and listening to soothing music can have calming effects that help the body and mind to relax. On the contrary, sleep deprivation can negatively impact your peace through mood disturbance and day-time loss of concentration, making it difficult for one to manage one's emotions and cope with daily stressors.

PUNCTUALITY & PEACE

I am meticulous about punctuality and most of us, including the ones reading this book are. Being late to events unsettles me, and I believe that habitual lateness does not benefit anyone's peace of mind.

LATENESS to work can make one feel stressed and unsettled, with loss of calm. Further loss of peace can result from pressure to catch up' in one's work that then creates grounds for troubling error. More so, continual lateness can impact one's self-esteem with loss of peace due to perceived or real stain on one's reputation.

While one, strictly speaking, may not go to hell for arriving late to work, forcing others to wait for us times after time is simply disrespectful, rude and unloving, and if there is an unrighteous motive to it, it can then be counted as sin. Also, continual lateness can be taken as insensitive because it disrupts others' plan and undermine their speed and momentum.

While not always intentional, habitual lateness which can frankly be perceived as discourteous and confrontational can create friction with tension that steals our PEACE. On the contrary, therefore, know punctuality and know peace.

PEACE IN COMPLETING TASKS OR ASSIGNMENTS

Backlog of uncompleted tasks can be overwhelming; sense of guilt that goes with missed targets can cause distress, and the cost of missed opportunities that go with procrastination, can lead to increased worry, stress and anxiety that can significantly affect peace of mind and overall well-being. This could be anything from unfinished course homework to missed upcoming presentation, or lapse in work-related office tasks, weight loss exercise schedule, family time meeting slot or other commitments. The list goes on and on.

Failure to keep to your plan or promise, particularly if this becomes a habit, can affect your mood and peace. The feeling of being behind in tasks and the frustration that goes with your unmet expectations of self, coupled with the negative consequences of failure to complete the tasks, can erode one's confidence or sense of accomplishment. Additionally, this can contribute to distrust in self with a feeling of helplessness undermining peace of mind.

Conversely, the successful completion of tasks and meeting expectations lead to a sense of satisfaction, positive self-image, confidence, contentment, and peace of mind.

BIG PEACE BOOSTERS

Big decisions are usually ones that border on major areas of our life and experience, including relationships, family, health, profession and finances. They have the advantage of attracting more attention, greater depth of effort, care or planning, and even large share of resources to get them managed.

This means the big decisions are often usually covered and usually not the trigger points for adversities that affects our peace.

This category encompasses all decisions or virtues aimed at salvation that influence our peace with both God and man.

LOVING & FORGIVING OTHERS

The unloving and unforgiving are like a person with a burden under a heavy weight and bereft of peace. But with love and forgiveness, your peace is guaranteed.

When you engage in actions that are driven by love for others, you are likely to respond with respect, kindness, care, empathy, patience and gentleness, all of which will inevitably lead to a state of peace of mind. When one is forgiving, offence will no longer be allowed to cause bitter rift with division that destroys the bond of love between two persons created in the image of God.

Love is a strong foundation for peace and unity. When love is reflected in daily life, it becomes a practical foundation for peace, and when what we do are motivated and inspired by our love for one another, we will treat others as we would like to be treated in a manner that richly fosters mutually beneficial and empowering relationship.

INTEGRITY

When your 'yes' is your 'yes' (Matthew 5:37), clarity is established, certainty is guaranteed, boundary is set and the reward is peace of mind.

The inspired integrity of a man guides and keeps him in peace for he walks in truth that's liberating (John 8:32) and fears no accusations, but whoever works in corruption or wickedness will not have peace (Isaiah 48:22)

Apostle Peter writes:

"Turn away from evil and do good. Search for peace, and work to maintain it. The eyes of the Lord watch over those who do right, and his ears are open to their prayers. But the Lord turns his face against those who do evil." (1 Peter 3:11-12 NLT).

DOING WHAT IS GOD

If anyone, then, knows the good they ought to do and doesn't do it, it is sin for them (James 4:17). When you do what is good as consistent with God's will, you will have your reward, of which peace **is one.**

"Now yield and submit yourself to Him [agree with God and be conformed to His will] and be at peace; In this way [you will prosper and great] good will come to you." (Job 22:21 AMP).

A FULFILLED MAN

A life defined by intentional work and grace-filled commitment to these big and small peace boosters is balanced and finds fulfilment as an unwavering steward in relationship with both God and man, as well as in service to God and man.

Such life is meticulous with discharge of its activities of daily living at home and in other places of service. He or she is good with boundary setting and task management, and comprehensive with calendar planning to ensure fail-safe execution of responsibilities to avert the risk of missed deadlines, missed appointments, failed promises and their likes which are potential stressors that can stifle peace.

A fulfilled man is uncompromising in salvation-based decisions, guided by inspired truth in the word (John 16:13).

When it comes to non-salvation-based decisions, a fulfilled man remaining committed to truth, eschews religion and yields to divine wisdom of James 3:17-18:

"But the wisdom from above is first of all pure (undefiled); then it is peace-loving, courteous (considerate, gentle). [It is willing to] yield to reason, full of compassion and good fruits; it is wholehearted and straightforward, impartial and unfeigned (free from doubts, wavering, and insincerity)." (James 3:17 AMPC).

Paul even encourages this wisdom in dispute situation (wherever it applies):

"Don't you realize that when you drag another believer into court you're providing the evidence that you are already defeated? Wouldn't it be better to accept the fact that someone is trying to cheat and take advantage of you, and simply choose the high road? At times it is better to just accept injustice and even to let someone take advantage of you, rather than to expose our conflicts publicly before unbelievers." (1 Corinthians 6:7 TPT).

An example is a "believing husband and a wife passing through a tense marital conflict, in custody battle over their children:

Paul is here saying that it would be better to make a positive compromise here instead of pyrrhic victory through a protracted court battle that may potentially impact the children negatively. It would be better to **let yourselves be cheated** than to desperately insist on achieving a particular goal, at the expense of the overall goof of the family, God's glory and the higher good of His kingdom.

Guided by the word, a fulfilled man will find inspiration through sanctified meditation on Philippians 4:8.

"And now, dear brothers and sisters, one final thing. Fix your thoughts on what is true, and honourable, and right, and pure, and lovely, and admirable. Think about things that are excellent and worthy of praise. Keep putting into practice all you learned and received from me—everything you heard from me and saw me doing. Then the God of peace will be with you." (Philippians 4:8-9 NLT)

"Therefore, let us pursue the things (big or small) which make for peace and the things by which one may edify another." (Romans 14:19 NKJV)

Chapter 12

PEACE ON ALL SIDES

Life should be viewed as an interconnected whole rather than isolated segments and achieving and maintaining peace across all areas of one's life is essential for a fulfilling, balanced and wholesome existence.

This above follows similar concept used in the inclusive definition of health by WHO (World Health Organisation).

World Health Organization (WHO) defines health as a state of complete physical, mental, and social well-being and not merely the absence of disease or infirmity (WHO, 1946). This definition encompasses a wide range of factors that influence health (including peace of mind, emotional and mental well-being, healthy and supportive environment) promoting a more comprehensive understanding of what it means to be healthy. By prioritizing well-being, the WHO encourages individuals and communities to engage in healthy behaviours and create supportive environments that foster health.

In the same way, the concept of multidimensional peace takes into consideration our desire and need for inner peace that is holistic, independent of external factors (**including our storms**) including our location (**our sterns**), occupation, and interpersonal relationships, as much as depends on us. A person who feels secure at home but lacks peace in other areas faces challenges. Similarly, an individual who is comfortable at work but apprehensive about returning home due to conflicts at home is also in a difficult situation. Life is beautiful but short, and it even becomes shorter for anyone whose life is bereft of peace of mind.

Achieving peace in all aspects of our lives is essential for productivity, whether at home, in relationships, or at the workplace. It is well-established that domestic situations can influence work performance, and experiences at work can affect one's sense of tranquillity at home. Therefore, it is imperative to pursue and maintain personal inner peace diligently and to safeguard it without compromise.

In 1 Kings 5:3, Solomon indicates that King David's official responsibilities were impacted by the absence of peace during his reign.

"You know that my father, David, was not able to build a Temple to honour the name of the LORD his God because of the many wars waged against him by surrounding nations. He could not build until the LORD gave him victory over all his enemies."

David could not build because he was fighting many wars with surrounding nations. It took some time before the LORD gave him victory over all his enemies. But Solomon's case was different. The LORD gave him peace (or rest) on every side, and he had no enemies and all was well.

Your productivity is dependent on the peace of your mind as well as sense of peace in what you do. Work for peace in your home, marriage, community, workplace and nation. Productivity is likely to be stalled, and many good things cannot be done in conflict or crisis time.

IS IT POSSIBLE TO HAVE PEACE ON ALL SIDES?

From a human perspective, this may seem unattainable, but from a spiritual standpoint, it is within the realm of possibility – as with God, all things are possible.

Luke 1:37 declares **"For with God nothing shall be impossible."**

Peace on all sides is possible; it is the gift of God, already covered in earlier chapters.

About the peace on all sides which the Lord gave him, Solomon speaks in 1 Kings 5:4: **"But now the Lord my God has given me peace on every side; I have no enemies, and all is well"** (NLT). Many translations use the word "rest" in place of peace.

WHAT CAN WE DO FOR PEACE ON ALL SIDES?

God, the prince of peace, has called us to live in peace with everyone. Hebrews 12:14 says we should pursue peace with all people. In other words, we should work at living in peace with everyone.

Similarly, Romans 12:18 says to do your part to live in peace with everyone, as much as possible.

"If it is possible, as much as depends on you, live peaceably with all men" (Romans 12:18 NKJV).

The scripture acknowledges the reality that mutual peace may not always be achievable due to circumstances beyond one's control. It therefore emphasizes personal responsibility in the pursuit of peace, suggesting that we should do everything within our power to seek peace and foster harmony. This aligns with the biblical teaching that, although God desires peace, human free will and sin create obstacles. In Matthew 5:9, Jesus blesses peacemakers, emphasizing peace as a valued pursuit in Christian life.

Peace on all sides is possible if:

- ❖ And when we cast our cares, burdens and worries upon God because He will take care of them all (1 Peter 5:7)
- ❖ We obey his command to not be anxious about anything, but in every situation, by prayer and petition, with thanksgiving, present our requests to God, so that His promised peace which transcends all understanding, will guard our hearts and our minds in Him (Philippians 4:6-7).
- ❖ We trust in the Lord with all our heart; lean not our own understanding and n all our ways acknowledge Him so He can direct us to the path of peace (Proverbs 3:5-6)
- ❖ We set our hearts steadfastly on Him

These will be possible when we:

- ➢ Seek first the kingdom of God and His righteousness so that all other things (including all forms of peace) shall be given to us (Matthew 6:38).
- ➢ Present ourselves and our bodies as living sacrifices, holy and acceptable to God; to truly worship Him with our lives, not conforming to the patterns of this world, but be transformed, with our minds renewed to fulfil God's perfect will (Romans 12:1-2).

- In submission to God, destroy every proud obstacle that keeps us from knowing Him and capture every rebellious idea, thoughts (including those of conflict and strife) making them obedient to God's command and will (1 Corinthians 10:4-6)

Peace on all sides is possible when we make **peace with God**, for then will we love Him as our God that we obey, who manifests in our lives (John 14:15-21). He them enables us to love our fellow humans as He loves us (John 13:34), making it possible for us to then have the kind of peace that God has **(peace of God)**, both with our creator (God) and with our neighbours (Humans, regardless of where we find ourselves **(our sterns)** and irrespective of the challenges that come our way **(our storms).**

May the peace of God, which surpasses all understanding guard your heart and mind through Christ Jesus as you read and digest the principles and revelations you receive through this book.

Amen!

REFERENCES

Bob and Debby Gass (2024) 'How to have peace', The UCB Word For Today, 12 June. Available at: http://www.ucb.co.uk/word-for-today/(Accessed 5 May 2025).

Cambridge dictionary (2025) Meaning of peace in Essential English Dictionary. Available at: https://dictionary.cambridge.org/dictionary/essential-british-english/peace/ (Accessed: February 3, 2025).

COMPSYCH (March 2027) Anxiety Skyrockets as Number One Presenting Issue Among American Workers Seeing Mental Health Assistance. Available at: https://www.compsych.com/press-release/anxiety-skyrockets-as-number-one-presenting-issue-among-american-workers-seeing-mental-health-assistance/ (Accessed: 29 February 2025).

COMPSYCH (May 2027) Anxiety Levels Soar Across UK Workforce According to New ComPsych Data. Available at: https://www.compsych.com/press-release/anxiety-levels-soar-across-uk-workforce-according-to-new-compsych-data/ (Accesses: 4 May, 2025).

Carnegie, D. (2006) *How to win friends and influence people: revised edition*. London: Vermillon.

Fletcher, J. (2024) 'Understanding how Nature and Nurture Influence Behaviour', PsychCentral, 2024. Available at: https://search.app/mFTf2wxacLaX34un9/ (Accessed: 15 April 2025)

Hardy, D. (2010). *The Compound effect: multiplying your success one simple step at a time*. Lake Dallas: Success Books.

James, K. (2023). *Legacy: what all blacks can teach us about the business of life*. London: Constable.

Healthline (2022). What is Mindfulness? A Simple Practice for Greater Well-being. Available at: https://www.healthline.com/health/mind—body/what-is-mindfulness#what-is-it (Accessed: 20 May 2025).

Patterson, K., Grenny, J., Maxfield, D., McMiillan, R. and Switzler, A. (2013) *Crucial Accountability.* New York: McGraw Hill Education.

Patterson, K., Grenny, J., Gregory, E., McMiillan, R. and Switzler, A. (2022) *Crucial Conversation*. New York: McGraw Hill Education.

Professional and Executive Development Harvard Division of continuing education (2023). Why Workplace Culture Matters. Available at: https://professional.dce.harvard.edu/blog/why-workplace-culture-matters/#What-is-Positive-Workplace-Culture (Accessed: 20 April 2025).

Wikipedia Contributors (2019). Stern. [online] Wikipedia. Available at: https://en.wikipedia.org/wiki/Stern/. (Accessed: 3 May 2025)

World Health Organisation (1946). Constitution of World Health Organisation. Available at: https://www.who.int/about/governance/constitution/ (Accessed: 3 June 2025).

ABOUT THE AUTHOR

Dr Ikechukwu Joshua Madumere is trained at the University of Nigeria and the Royal College of General Practitioners, holding postgraduate qualifications in Public Health from the University of East London and in Frailties from the University of Kent.

As an ordained minister and church leader within The Redeemed Christian Church of God, he holds pastoral responsibility at City of David Parish in Canterbury.

Ikechukwu is dedicated to promoting healthy relationships and righteous living, especially in marriage. As a Counsellor, Evangelist, teacher, motivational speaker, and Church Trustee of RCCG Living Faith South Shields and RCCG Living Glory Birmingham, he has inspired many with his messages and leadership.

He is a dedicated worshiper and recreational, private singer who values fellowship with various Christian communities. He actively participates in the Overseas Fellowship of Nigerian Christians (OFNC) and engages with colleagues, friends, and fellow believers of all races and ethnicities.

Ikechukwu was born in Umunze, Anambra State, Nigeria, and currently resides in Canterbury, United Kingdom with his wife, Chinelo, and their children: Joshua, David, Caleb, and Chizara.

You can read more about Ikechukwu's ministry on his Facebook page: https://www.facebook.com/THLVision/

RESOURCES FROM THE AUTHOR

A God-centred, love-driven guide to a lasting marriage.

In *The Beauty of Relationship - Focus on Marriage*, Dr Ikechukwu Joshua Madumere draws on biblical truths, real-life experiences, and over a decade of marital wisdom to help couples thrive. Whether you're single, engaged, or married, this book equips you to build a relationship rooted in love, trust, unity, and God's original design for marriage.

You may download your copy from here: https://www.amazon.co.uk/BEAUTY-RELATIONSHIP-Focus-Marriage-ebook/dp/B0816YK9K/

Printed in Dunstable, United Kingdom

66126228R00100